FEAST ❖

Also by Christina Rees

The Divine Embrace

Sea Urchin

Voices of this Calling

FEAST ✤ FAST

FOOD FOR
LENT AND EASTER

CHRISTINA
REES

DARTON · LONGMAN + TODD

First published in 2010 by
Darton, Longman and Todd Ltd
1 Spencer Court
140–142 Wandsworth High Street
London SW18 4JJ

ISBN: 978-0-232-52844-2

A catalogue record for this book is available from the British Library.

Designed and typeset by Judy Linard
Printed and bound in Great Britain by Page Brothers, Norwich, Norfolk

For Chris
with gratitude and love

For everything there is a season

and a time for every matter under heaven:

a time to be born, and a time to die;

a time to plant, and a time to pluck up what is planted;

a time to kill, and a time to heal;

a time to break down, and a time to build up;

a time to weep, and a time to laugh;

a time to mourn, and a time to dance;

a time to throw away stones, and a time to gather stones together;

a time to embrace, and a time to refrain from embracing;

a time to seek, and a time to lose;

a time to keep, and a time to throw away;

a time to tear, and a time to sew;

a time to keep silence, and a time to speak;

a time to love, and a time to hate;

a time for war, and a time for peace.

ECCLESIASTES 3:1–9

CONTENTS

ACKNOWLEDGEMENTS

I am grateful to so many people for their help and encouragement with this book. First of all, I would like to thank Virginia Hearn, Commissioning Editor at Darton, Longman and Todd, who suggested the idea for this book and who has been a steady and constant support. It has been a great pleasure working with Virginia and some of the other lovely people at Darton, Longman and Todd, including Helen Porter, Will Parkes and Aude Pasquier. Kathy Dyke deserves special thanks for taking some of my rather 'free style' recipes and ensuring they were all consistent and coherent.

I am deeply grateful to everyone who contributed some of their best-loved recipes with such enthusiasm for the food and for the project. My daughters, Angela and Alex Rees, both gave me recipes and, in addition, Alex contributed fresh ideas about nutrition and eating well. I have to say that they also teased me mercilessly about having to measure the ingredients for my recipes, having watched me for years just throwing meals together!

Several recipes use cup measurements; measuring cups are available from Amazon, John Lewis, online retailers and good cookware stores.

I am particularly grateful to my sister, Robin Muller Perez, not only for her own recipes, but also for rediscovering some favourite recipes which our mother, Carol Benton Muller, had collected and created years ago, and which had been buried in boxes of old books and papers. My sister-in-law, Keri Ataumbi Muller, responded from the wilds of Santa Fe with some delicious and unusual recipes that she and my brother Joel enjoy.

I also had wonderful responses from my cousins Kathy Muller Noble, Peggy Muller Bjarno and Crystal Woodward. Crystal's brother Eric Woodward and his wife Hilary contributed indirectly through their daughter Emma, who happily came for a visit while I was writing this book, along with her friends Juliana Duryea and Genevieve Spellman, during their epic cycling tour of Europe. Emma and her friends concocted a delicious fruit compote and Gen gave me an entirely raw food recipe.

I have also used recipes from other family members no longer with us: my paternal grandparents, John Muller and Olga Popoff Muller, and my mother-in law, Margaret Rees. I am sorry I was not able to collect recipes from all the members of my extended family, but this exercise has inspired me to pursue more pooling of recipes and the various traditions connected with celebrations and feasts.

Other friends whose recipes I have used, and to whom I am immensely grateful, include Aaqil Ahmed, Alice Baldwin, Michelle Desault, Myrna Grant, Sue Jagelman, Cuptal Johnson, Jean Longdin, Barbara Ludlow, Sarah Smith, Jenny Standage and Leon Wambsganss. I also owe special thanks to Christopher and Sally Kevill-Davies: to Sally for her helpful information on the subject of food eaten during Lent in times past, and to Christopher for various other historical nuggets! I would like to thank Jenny Simmons for her most helpful information on macrobiotic cooking – so much more could have been written on that subject.

Last, but very much not least, I would like to thank my husband Chris, for his delicious casserole recipe (and for the many wonderful meals he cooks!), for his ceaseless technological help and for all his support and the partnership we share. It is to him this book is dedicated.

Christina Rees
OCTOBER 2010

INTRODUCTION

It may seem odd to write about fasting and feasting in the same book, but our lives are lived in cycles and seasons. The time of Lent involves both the practice of abstinence and the preparation for abundance. The great celebration of Easter calls for our best response to the miracle of new life.

Lent is also a time for reflection, penitence and re-appraisal. It is a time for giving over a greater part of one's heart and mind and soul to a closer attention to things of the spirit. Few of us, however, can remove ourselves from our normal daily lives and cloister ourselves in places where we will not be distracted from spiritual thoughts and disciplines. One of the ironies of Lent is that, if we attend Lent courses and read Lent books (such as this one!), it can feel as if even more is being loaded onto us, more activities added to our already over-crowded lives. And yet, in the meeting together with others to consider more deeply what it means to follow the way of Christ, we may meet with Christ himself and enter into his peace. In the reading of simple, familiar words, we may gain new insights into the eternal mystery of God.

Lent involves our sticking with the inexorable journey Jesus took to the cross, and thinking again what that means to us, as well as holding the awareness that Easter follows Good Friday, new life follows death, and reflecting on the nature of that new life. Some of the raw ingredients of Lent are remembering and regretting, longing and letting go, planning and praying. These things do not only imply a spiritual, intellectual or emotional engagement, but a physical one as well. Paradoxically, as we practise acts and rituals of self-denial, of refraining from things which give us physical pleasure, instead of resulting in the shutting down of our sensory experience and awareness, the season of Lent can be a time for reconnecting with the senses, for discovering in new ways an appreciation of what it means to be an embodied physical being.

For many of us, gaining such an appreciation will involve slowing down, doing less and becoming more mindful of the daily routine. If nothing else, Lent is a time for *mindfulness* in all that we do. This may require taking more care with food and mealtimes and all the work and activity that goes into that – the shopping, preparing, cooking and eating, even the clearing up. It may prompt us to shed certain assumptions and habits, or at least make us willing to reconsider them. Lent can help us to see ourselves and the stuff of our lives in a different light.

In Lent, we are called to travel back in time, back to first-century Palestine, where we walk with others along dusty roads and sit on grassy hills and listen again to the words of the Teacher. We are also called to travel forward in our imagination, to times and things we long for, to the brighter realisation of dreams and visions as yet unrealised.

In Lent, if we let ourselves, we can splash in refreshing fountains and bask in the warmth of Divine love. We can allow the light of

Christ to shine into the shadowy corners of our hearts and minds with its transforming, healing light. Spring cleaning is not just for the dust and mould and grime in our houses, but also for our hearts and minds and bodies and souls!

There are so many different patterns and traditions associated with Lent, but for most of us, there are few set rules. Some people give up certain things each year, like alcohol, chocolate or meat, and others incorporate new practices, such as reading the Bible, attending a Lent course or fasting, but there is no one fixed way of observing Lent. The goal and the purpose is to walk more closely with perhaps the only 'rule' necessary for a Lent that has the potential for bringing us closer to God; the willingness to be as honest as possible with yourself and with God.

There is so much that can be said about the time of Lent and the momentous events in Jesus' life that took place particularly in the week leading up to his death and resurrection. I cannot possibly cover the vast range of important topics that are part of this season in the Christian calendar: that is not the purpose of this book. Rather, what I hope is that this book may act as a little catalyst to help you to enter into the season of Lent in ways that will be meaningful and relevant to you.

I have included a section on fasting, because it is something I have done for most of my life. In fact, as I explain in this book, I was introduced to fasting perhaps earlier than I would have liked to have been! I have found fasting to be an extraordinary way of cutting through the clutter and cacophony of my thoughts and preoccupations, allowing me to give more attention to the still, small voice of the Spirit, and allowing my body a respite from the work of digesting and processing food. It goes without saying that if you are planning on fasting and you have any conditions that require medical attention, you should first check with your doctor.

I am deeply indebted to all those who provided their tried and tested recipes, some of which have been used and loved for many decades. I have tried to include only those which use wholesome, nutritious ingredients and which are fairly easy to prepare. I do, of course, allow for a little bit of spoiling on Sundays and Easter! My own style of cooking is to use fresh food and to prepare it as simply as possible. I am definitely more in the free-form style of Jamie Oliver rather than the more intricate Raymond Blanc style of cooking!

I have learned that many people have certain recipes that hold potent memories of much-loved family members. Eating specific dishes can provide strong reconnections with loved ones and with past times. I am grateful also to those who spoke with me about how they approached the whole subject of eating and cooking during the season of Lent. I have become much more aware of the different ways in which people use Lent as a time of spiritual and physical thoughtfulness, as a time set apart for the renewal of hearts and minds and bodies. However Lent is approached, I pray this season you may discover more of the God who has walked our human path and who still walks with us and in us.

PREPARING
FOR LENT

Don't you know that you are God's temple and that God's Spirit dwells in you?

1 CORINTHIANS 3:16

God gives power to the faint,
and strengthens the powerless.
Even youths will faint and be weary and young men will fall
    exhausted;
but those who wait for the Lord shall renew their strength,
they shall mount up with wings like eagles,
they shall run and not be weary,
they shall walk and not faint.

ISAIAH 40:29–31

Put me to the test, says the Lord of hosts, if I will not open the windows of heaven
for you and pour down for you an overflowing blessing.

MALACHI 3:10

Ask, and you will be given what you ask for. Seek, and you will find. Knock, and the
door will be opened. For everyone who asks, receives. Anyone who seeks, finds. If
only you will knock, the door will be opened.

MATTHEW 7:7–8

THINKING ABOUT FOOD

It is heartbreaking to see how so many people's relationship with food has become disordered in some way. Either we eat too much, or not enough. Some of us disdain all foods except those of which we approve, and some of us eat anything without caring what it will do to our bodies and our overall health and wellbeing. Collectively, we waste and throw away mountains of food a year, and yet we spend millions of pounds on diet food and diet products. We have turned the very stuff we need to survive and thrive into a problem or an obsession.

In the past in some traditions it was thought that a negative or lazy attitude towards taking care of oneself was the root cause of all disease. Some Christians believed that disease and ill health were caused by the accumulation of negative thoughts and emotions, which drew even more negative energy to a person's body until they became ill. Now we know so much more about diseases and illnesses, but it is certainly the case that how we view our bodies and respect their needs and what we feed ourselves affects our health and sense of wellbeing. It is now acknowledged and recognised by the medical world that stress, anxiety, overwork, grief and unresolved anger can cause as much, if not more, damage to our health than a poor diet.

Babies and young children are refreshingly, and sometimes embarrassingly, honest about their bodily needs. When they are hungry, they cry for food. When they are tired, they go to sleep. As adults, we may need to redevelop the practice of being aware of what our bodies are communicating to us. How often do we become irritated by our bodies when they become hungry or tired? How dismissive are we of our bodies' genuine needs?

We may experience low self-esteem or feel unworthy at times, and we must not let those emotions, which seem to be an occasional part of almost everyone's life, spill over into neglecting our bodies or not caring about the food we eat. Our bodies deserve as much love and care as do our hearts and minds and spirits. Becoming mindful involves not only being mindful of our thoughts and emotions, but also mindful about everything we eat and drink.

Some people eat too much because eating feels so good. It is satisfying and comforting. Also, a duvet of fat around the body can both protect and conceal. One of the challenges for people who overeat in order to hide beneath their fat is to discover how they can learn to feel safe without an extra layer of fat. Some people who have lost a large amount of weight describe feeling vulnerable, a sense of no longer having anywhere to hide. Instead of hating our bodies, we should recognise the ways they have reacted to our thoughts and emotions and realise that they have only done their best to respond to what we have been communicating to them.

We are told that our bodies respond to every thought we think and every emotion we feel. The King James Version of the Bible has wise old Solomon saying, 'As a man thinketh, so he is' (Proverbs 23:7), making a direct connection between our thoughts and who we are. We cannot get away from the fact that eating healthy food creates healthy bodies; it also helps to create healthy hearts and minds. Eating food that is good for us is another way of treating ourselves with love and self-respect.

I know of many people, including myself, who have used the period of Lent as a time for reassessing their overall health and fitness. In my view that is entirely appropriate. Taking care of our bodies and being the right weight is honouring both to ourselves and to God. It is commendable to want to be healthier, but it is important to be honest about what one is doing and why one is doing it. If your goal is to lose ten pounds during the 40 days of Lent, then be clear about your goal and dedicate your desire to God. Being unfit and unhealthy when you can do something about it is not honouring either to yourself or to God.

Why should going on a diet in order to lose extra weight be any less a worthy discipline and activity than building in a time of prayer and reflection every day? If we can learn to see ourselves – all the elements and aspects of who we are – as being of importance, then we will perhaps be less likely to split off what we think and believe about God from how we treat our bodies.

Many of us would never think of being unkind or cruel to someone, yet we feed our bodies with food that does not nourish us and we allow our bodies to become unfit. I know, because I've done it myself. The truth is our bodies are very much part of who we are, and are absolutely necessary to us during our lives here on planet earth. We skip meals and grab snacks that cannot nourish our vital organs – and then we wonder why we feel so flat, so depressed, so lacklustre. We are shocked when things start to go wrong inside us after decades of neglect and abuse.

Everyone in the Western world is aware of the dangers of

smoking, of drinking too much alcohol and of eating certain types of food, yet we ignore the cumulative effects of depriving our bodies of the nutrients they need to function properly while overloading them with toxins and substances that our bodies were never intended to consume.

Lent can be an exercise in letting go of aspects of our lives that have become unnecessary and unhelpful. Try to see whatever Lenten discipline you choose as being not only an opportunity for self-denial, but also an opportunity of ridding yourself of all the accretions that are obscuring who you really are. What habits and patterns, whether of the body, heart or mind, have you developed which are preventing you from being all that you have been created to be? Part of dying to self is dying to false views of yourself that have no place in the life of a beloved child of God. Jesus said that he came so that we might enjoy life in all its abundance – to the full, till it overflows! (John 10:10). His desire for us is that we will live so completely in his joy that the cup of our joy will overflow! (John 15:11).

One of the paradoxes of following Christ is that we can have peace and joy even when we are in the middle of difficult circumstances. Such things are fruits of the Spirit, as Paul wrote to the Galatians. They grow in us as we abide in Christ, and like any fruit, if the conditions are right, they will grow. In addition to joy and peace, other fruits of the Spirit are love, patience, kindness, goodness, faithfulness, gentleness and self-control. Lent is probably a good time to observe how these fruit are growing in the garden of your spirit!

Take delight in the LORD, and he will give you the desires of your heart.

PSALM 37:4

The Story of the Willow Tree

One morning when I was still half asleep I heard a loud cracking noise from outside. It was the sound of a great splintering, as if a huge tree was crashing down in our garden. The biggest tree we have is an old willow tree, growing not far from the corner of our house near our bedroom. I threw on some clothes and ran outside and was shocked to discover a large willow branch, well over a foot in diameter, lying under the willow tree, as if snapped off by a bad-tempered passing giant.

I could make no sense of it. One minute the tree had been fine, the next minute a huge branch had just snapped through and fallen off. It could not have been lightning, because there was no storm. It could not have been disease, because the base of the branch looked healthy. The broken branch was lying right over the path by our house, so Chris asked a neighbour with a chain saw to come and help him remove the branch, chunk by chunk.

Our neighbour knew of a tree expert, who came up the next day to look at our tree and try to solve the mystery of the fallen branch. It didn't take him long to figure out what had happened. It turns out that willows and virtually all other trees, as well as many other things in nature, operate within certain laws. One of these laws is the *axiom of uniform stress*. The axiom of uniform stress is about how a system, in this instance, a tree, behaves in order to keep as strong and efficient as possible.

A tree is a finely balanced and complex system. In order to survive, it has to maintain its balance, and in order to do that it must not become too heavy or lopsided. There is an element in the bark called cambium which is the 'brains' of the tree. Cambium can sense where there is undue stress and respond by either increasing or decreasing growth. Evidently, the brains of our willow must have decided it was out of balance in a certain area and so the tree just 'let go' of a branch in order to rebalance itself.

I expect there are many ways in which humans also follow the axiom of uniform stress, making innumerable conscious and subconscious decisions that help to keep our lives in balance. Sometimes, no doubt, like the willow tree, we resort to drastic measures and find ways of making changes that will bring us back into equilibrium.

Something that happened to another tree in the garden taught me another lesson. Last autumn, one of our old apple tree began to lean over because of the weight of its fruit and the direction of the strong prevailing winds. One day I went outside to discover the tree lying on the ground! The main roots were still intact, but it had not been able to stay upright any longer. Even though it looked healthy and was clearly producing a great crop of fruit, it had got out of balance and did not have the strength to remain standing. If only I had realised that the tree was getting so unbalanced, I could have propped up its branches and given it the support it needed. The apples still ripened, but the tree needed drastic pruning and we never managed to get it back fully upright.

In all your ways acknowledge him, and he will make straight your paths.

PROVERBS 3:6

FOR FURTHER THOUGHT
- What in your life do you think may be out of balance?
- What can you do to help restore your equilibrium?
- Will you need help from anyone else?

FOR PRAYER
- Pray for people who cannot see any way out of their present situation. Pray that they may be given hope, a fresh vision and the means to make changes.
- Pray for the children and partners of people whose lives are out of balance for whatever reason.

FOR FURTHER READING
- Psalm 86
- John 15
- Galatians 5:22–23

MINDFULNESS

If you do nothing else this season of Lent, becoming more mindful about how you live – how you shop, cook, and eat, the other things you buy and the media you imbibe – would be worthwhile in itself.

Mindfulness involves intentional thought and action and includes being aware of our thoughts and emotions, as well as being spiritually alert and aware. It also involves being attuned to our bodies and how they are feeling. It is extraordinary how out of touch we can be with our own bodies and how deaf we can be to the messages they are trying to communicate to us.

If we are to become more mindful, then we may have to slow down, and if we are going to slow down, we almost certainly will have to do less. There is a lovely concept that my friend Claire Pedrick, the director of 3D Coaching, told me about. It is called 'planned neglect', and it forms part of the Rule of Life by the Companions of Brother Lawrence. Planned neglect entails making a deliberate choice about the 'things we will leave undone or postpone, so that instead of being oppressed by a clutter of unfinished jobs, we think out our priorities under God, and then accept, without guilt or resentment, the fact that much we had thought we ought to do, we must leave' (*Rule of Life*, Companions of Brother Lawrence).

Planned neglect can be as much a part of being mindful as planned attention. The important thing is to make a conscious choice and then let go of whatever it is you have decided not to do, or give your attention to whatever it is you have decided to do. Being more mindful can help to prevent the subtle build-up of mental and emotional silt, the anxiety and fretting that can rob us of all joy and lead us to believe that we have no choice or say in our circumstances.

There are many things that can make us feel as if we are out of control, as if we have somehow strayed into someone else's life and drama, that we are passive passengers along for the ride. Although some of us may have been victims of various circumstances and crimes, such as discrimination, abuse, neglect, robbery or rape, in our inner being and with help, we do not have to remain forever as victims. There is hope, even in cases of the most appalling brutality and inhumanity.

Organisations like the Medical Foundation work with victims of torture, and help to bring people back from utter despair and desolation. There may be permanent scars – physical, emotional and mental – but in all but the most extreme cases, the ability of the human spirit to overcome terrible acts of cruelty and violence is astonishing. I am often completely overawed and silenced by the courage and resilience of people who have been through unimaginable horrors, from the survivors of the concentration camps in World War II, to the survivors of the Rwandan genocide, to those who have been caught up in acts of terror or freak accidents. Thankfully, most of us will never experience such extreme traumas, but hearing the stories of those who have tell us something about who we really are and what we are made of. We are rarely as impotent as we may feel.

Part of Jesus' teaching was about the immense power we possess. As he said to his disciples, 'truly I tell you, if you say to this mountain, "Be taken up and thrown in to the sea", and if you do not doubt in your heart, but believe that what you say will come to pass, it will be done for you. So I tell you, whatever you ask for in prayer, believe that you have received it, and it will be yours' (Mark 11:23–24). The message is that what we believe, we will receive.

When the various women in the crowds used to come up to Jesus and touch his robe, believing that if they even touched his clothing they would be healed, he would always say to them that it was their faith that had made them well. When we bend our hearts and minds and wills to something, there is little that can stop us, and Jesus made it explicit that there is great power in the asking when we ask in faith.

> Do not withhold good from those to whom it is due, when it is in your power to do it.
>
> PROVERBS 3:27

FOR FURTHER THOUGHT
- What would feed your spirit and soul? How can you bring that into your life?
- Ask yourself before buying anything, do I really need this? If you don't, think about what else you could do with the money. At the end of Lent, use the money you've saved to buy something that will help you to live a more healthy and integrated life, or donate it to a cause you care about, or give it to someone who needs it more than you do.

- What in your life most needs a spring clean?

FOR PRAYER
- Pray for people who have lost hope.
- Pray for children and young people who are not given the love and care they need.
- Pray for help in discovering what you need to give up or take on.

FOR FURTHER READING
- Psalm 104
- Isaiah 35
- Matthew 6:19–24

EATING WELL

Unless you are already spending a minimal amount on food, it may be possible to cut the cost of food during Lent. Are there things you routinely buy that you could do without? How much money could you save if you decided to spend a tenth less on your weekly food bill? Of course, with children it's important to have plenty of good food in the house, but even if you have children, might it be possible to cut out some foods that may have started out as treats and now become habits? See the checklist 'Rules of Thumb for Healthy Eating' on p.36, and think about changes you might be able to incorporate within your Lenten routine.

Vegetarianism

According to the Vegetarian Society (www.vegsoc.org), about a tenth of the population of the United Kingdom is vegetarian. Among adults, it's about 7 per cent and among young people it goes up to 12 per cent. Many more people are choosing to eat significantly less meat and if the trend continues at its present rate, England one day will be a largely vegetarian country.

There are a number of compelling reasons for being vegetarian, quite apart from the ethical reason of not wanting to contribute to the suffering of animals. Vegetarians have less heart disease and lower blood pressure than meat eaters and there are many fewer obese vegetarians.

In a world where so many people do not have enough to eat, I find it somewhat disturbing that 80 per cent of all agricultural land in the United Kingdom is used to rear livestock and almost 50 per cent of all cereal crops grown in Britain are used as animal feed. Having said all that, I am not a vegetarian. I do eat less meat but I still eat it. For years I even kept a flock of Soay sheep just so I could feed my children healthy meat. I expect, however, that in centuries to come there will be fewer animals reared for food and more grains grown for human consumption. I seriously question whether the current situation is sustainable in the long term.

I think many people are aware of a dissonance, as I am, between wanting to eat meat and yet also wanting to ensure that there is enough good food for other people, and also wanting to care for animals and the planet. For vegetarians and for those who choose not to eat meat during Lent, I have included a number of vegetarian recipes. Also, many of the recipes which list meat as an ingredient can easily be made vegetarian by replacing the meat with another vegetable or a food such as tofu or Quorn.

Macrobiotic or Raw Food Diets

Another way of eating in Lent could be to adopt an entirely different approach to food, such as following a macrobiotic or raw food diet, even if just for one day a week. Macrobiotic cooking is based on the traditional Japanese diet and emphasises the importance of balance in eating. 'Macro' means 'big' or 'large' in Greek, and 'biotic' has to do with life, so macrobiotic cooking is about a holistic view of eating and living.

There are many books and websites devoted to macrobiotic cooking and you can quickly decide if this approach is something you might wish to try. There is also the Macrobiotic Association of Great Britain (www.macrobiotics.org.uk), which has lots of information and some wonderful recipes! Eating a macrobiotic diet has been known to help people to lose weight, control diabetes, lower high blood pressure and cholesterol and help with many other ailments. Macrobiotic cooking can take a while to get used to, but the principles are simple – eat as locally and seasonally as possible and eat more grains and vegetables than meat and dairy foods.

There are some people who *only* eat raw food, but I can't imagine doing that myself, especially during the colder months. The thinking behind this way of eating is that when food is cooked, inevitably some of the enzymes and nutrients are destroyed, so by eating food in its natural state, you get more of the nutritional benefits. Genevieve Spellman, a recent guest in my house during her European cycling tour, is a young woman in her early 20s who ate only raw food for a year and a half. During that time, she said she had much more energy and felt more in touch with her body. She came off the strict raw food diet, however, when she decided to embark on the cycling tour!

If you would like to give your system a rest from processed or rich food, eating raw food is an easy and effective way to do it. Try eating just fruit and vegetables for a day. Start the day with an apple or two, or juice a variety of raw fruit and vegetables. You can also eat dried fruit and nuts for extra energy. One of my favourite lunches is to juice a few sticks of celery, half a cucumber, a couple of apples or pears, a lemon, a lime and a large piece of fresh ginger root – delicious! If you like the idea of eating raw food, you can also try the recipe for lasagne that Gen gave me (see p. 131), which is enough to convert anyone to raw food, if only for an occasional meal!

Obesity

Another scandal is the growing number of seriously overweight children in the Western world, especially in the United States, but also increasingly in Britain. It is known that a bad diet in childhood leads to long-term health problems, yet now, according to the National Child Measurement Programme, more than one in five children who start school in the United Kingdom are already overweight or obese. In her article 'Young, Loaded and Green', Jessica Brinton notes that it is an ironic tragedy that obesity is now the second largest killer in the Western world (*Sunday Times*, 25 July 2010).

The celebrity chef Jamie Oliver has a passion for helping to ensure that children are provided with good healthy food. On both sides of the Atlantic, Jamie has been spreading his message of healthy eating for children and working with politicians, educationalists and people in the medical profession to help bring an end to what is an entirely preventable problem. Jamie's vision is 'to educate every child about food, inspire families to cook again and empower people everywhere to fight obesity' (*Sunday Times*, 25 July 2010).

In order to be healthy and function properly, our bodies need protein, some carbohydrates and a little bit of fat. Our muscles are the building blocks of our bodies and protein is the cement that keeps them together. The fat we eat should primarily be vegetable fat, like olive oil or the fat in avocados. Eggs are brilliant, because they are a good source of protein and essential fatty acids.

The exact amount of carbohydrates we need and the role they play in weight loss is still disputed. Try to ensure the carbohydrates you eat are low-GI. (GI is the glycaemic index, which measures the conversion rate of starch (carbohydrate) to glucose.) Good sources of low-GI carbohydrates are porridge, wholemeal bread and baked beans.

We really don't need sugar, and certainly no refined sugar, but avoiding it is extremely difficult. I try only to eat sugar I really love, like the sugar in fresh and dried fruits and the occasional piece of dark chocolate. Of course, for special occasions, I eat it and enjoy it and then go back to my normal routine of avoiding it.

One of the problems for people trying to lose weight is that when we cut down on calories, our metabolic rate slows down and our bodies start to conserve energy, thereby slowing down the amount of calories we burn. That's why sometimes people who barely eat anything still hardly lose any weight. It takes a combination of eating the right types of food with enough calories and exercise to take off weight and keep it off.

RULES OF THUMB FOR HEALTHY EATING

- Try to cut out processed foods.
- If you can't grow it or kill it, don't eat it.
- If you are going to feel bad about eating something, don't eat it.
- If something has a great long list of ingredients, and you don't recognise most of them as food, don't eat it.
- If you don't know what it is, don't eat it.
- Don't be afraid of feeling hungry between meals. Most people in the West don't know what hunger feels like.
- Don't eat in front of the TV.
- Don't bring books, mobiles or iPhones to the table.
- Stimulating our tastes buds makes us want to eat more. The greater variety of different tastes there are in one meal, the hungrier we will feel.
- If you feel thirsty you're already dehydrated. A lot of people are chronically thirsty. Often we mistake thirst for hunger. Try drinking a glass of water or having a cup of herbal tea. If you are still hungry, then eat some food.
- Many people are busy and stressed. It seems we are all time-poor. Try to eat one meal a day with your family. Even if it's only a few meals a week, eat together.
- Try to make eating food a celebration to share with your family and friends. I often bemoan the fact that one of the greatest losses for Gentile Christians was to drop the Jewish tradition of families and extended families coming together for the weekly Shabbat meal. Some people I know carry on a version of this tradition by always having a cooked meal at Sunday lunchtime and inviting family and friends to join them at their table. It is heartbreaking

that so many people in our culture are lonely, and yet, if they knew they would be welcome at someone's table once a week, their lives would be significantly happier. Who could you invite for a meal?

- If it's appropriate, take turns cooking with the other people you live with. If you have children at home, involve them in cooking, and not just the cooking, but planning the menus and rotating the different tasks connected with preparing, serving and cleaning up after meals.
- Take a walk after a meal. Identify whether you are a lark or an owl, and plan your exercise accordingly. Fit it in when you can. Exercise can be fun, but everyone is different, so do what suits you. If you have Wii Fit, you can play tennis, basketball, golf or other sports. Play with someone in the family or with a friend. Grandparents can play with grandchildren.

We like food because we need it. The things that give us pleasure tend to be the things we need to survive. We need to pay attention to the physical aspects of our existence and honour them as we do the emotional, intellectual and spiritual aspects of our lives.

Remember, it won't be possible to make all the changes we want all at once, because change is usually a process. Of course, some changes can be transacted in a moment, but most take place over a period of time. The more positive we can be about the changes we either have to, or want to, make, the better it will be. Resisting change creates stress, which is a recipe for illness. We need to remind ourselves that if we have begun the process and remain committed to it, then no setbacks can properly be called failures. As long as we are keeping faith with the process, we are learning and changing.

Anything you undertake as part of a Lenten ritual, anything you decide to change, should be done in the light of knowing yourself to be loved by God. Nothing can be done or needs to be done in an attempt to win God's approval. God loves each and every one of us with non-stop, never-ending, unconditional love. By all means eat healthier food, read the Bible more, take up exercise and be more kind to your neighbours – these are all good things, but you do not have to do any of it to win God's love. Like the sun shining above the clouds, God's love is there, all the time. God's love is. How we respond is up to us.

SLEEPING WELL

Many of us treat ourselves in ways we would never treat anyone else – not even, perhaps not especially, a beloved pet. When our children are hungry we feed them. When our dog or cat or budgie is hungry, we feed them. We make sure they have adequate exercise, and we are careful not to push them to exhaustion. We provide them with comfortable beds and we do not ridicule them for needing to sleep. We would certainly never routinely deprive them of the sleep they need, forcing them to stay awake when they were clearly exhausted.

Yet many of us push our bodies in ways that would be considered cruel if we were animals. We override our need for sleep and keep ourselves awake with unhealthy stimulants. Even natural stimulants like coffee, tea and chocolate become unhealthy if overused. We boast about how late we can stay up working. We joke that sleep is for wimps, but it is clear that's precisely what we think. There is a wonderful verse in the Psalms that addresses this negative tendency, showing us that it is not only part of our contemporary condition: 'It is in vain you get up earlier and put off going to bed, sweating to make a living; for God gives sleep to his beloved' (Psalm 127:2). If the only thing you changed this Lent was to make sure you got enough sleep, think of how it might transform how you feel!

Look upon eating healthy food not as an indulgence, but as a way of showing gratitude to God for giving you this life. By eating good food and following healthy patterns of sleeping and exercise, you can help to maintain good health or bring your body back to health. It may be a cliché, but that doesn't stop it from being true: each day is a new opportunity. We don't have yesterday any more and we don't yet have tomorrow, but we do have today.

Years ago I was taught a catchy saying to remind me of this truth – *there's power in the present*. Say it to yourself a few times a day until you believe it! There is power in the present. In a sense, there is only power in the present. Each day when we wake up we can make a fresh start by being grateful for all we have been given, and we can thank and praise God for being God. I was also taught another saying: *there's power in praise*. Even in the midst of difficult circumstances that we desperately want to change, we can still praise God for the good there is in our lives and we can always be thankful for God's unstoppable love for us.

DRINKING WELL

Another change we could make that would reap positive benefits for our bodies and minds, is to make sure we drink enough water. Our bodies are about 70 per cent water. Our blood is mainly composed of water. Our internal organs need water to function properly. If we don't drink enough water we become dehydrated. While it's quite difficult to become seriously dehydrated (that is, to lose more than 10 per cent of fluid from our bodies), it is not uncommon to become mildly dehydrated just by forgetting to drink enough during the day. Symptoms of mild dehydration can include a raised heart rate and temperature, more rapid breathing, muscle cramps, headaches, nausea and extreme fatigue and weakness. Luckily, symptoms of mild dehydration disappear fairly quickly when we drink water or other fluids. Getting severely dehydrated, however, is very dangerous and even life-threatening, and is the tragic reality for thousands of people who do not have access to safe drinking water.

If you live in a place where you have access to fresh, clean drinking water, then you are fortunate indeed. If you can access the water with a turn of a tap, then you are even more fortunate. According to the organisation water.org (www.water.org) founded by Matt Damon and Gary White, even in the twenty-first century nearly one billion people do not have access to safe drinking water. That's about one in eight people who are forced to drink water that is not safe. As a result of this dreadful situation, over 3.5 million people die each year from water-related diseases. Nearly 1.5 million children die each year from water-related diseases. Diarrhoea is currently the second leading cause of death among children under five, and it is directly related to drinking unhygienic water. Diarrhoea kills more young children under five than malaria, AIDS and measles combined.

Half of the beds in hospitals around the world are occupied by people with water-related diseases. Even the ancient Romans had better access to safe drinking water than half of the people alive now. Like many conditions around the globe, the lack of safe drinking water has a particular effect on women, as it is women who traditionally collect and carry water for their families and livestock.

Every day, more than 200 million hours of women's time is spent collecting water. Providing enough water, a basic necessity of life, is for too many women a task that effectively prevents them from staying in education or employment. For these women it is a case of the poor staying poor. Two thirds of the people who do not have access to safe drinking water survive on less than $2 a day, and one third survive on less than $1 a day. There are many charities that help to ensure people have access to safe drinking water. Perhaps you could stop buying water during Lent and give the money you save to a charity that provides safe drinking water for people who have none, or that works to improve sanitation for people.

Meanwhile, we can remind ourselves of all the ways to conserve water that we've been taught since we were children: turn off the tap while we brush our teeth, run off the water we need into a bowl to do the washing up, use dishwashers only when they are full or switch back to washing up by hand; and remember, a five-minute shower uses more water than many people have access to for an entire day.

> But strive first for the kingdom of God; and his righteous-
> ness, and all these things will be given to you as well.
>
> MATTHEW 6:33

LIVING WELL

Our bodies need to move in order to be healthy and work properly, but according to the NHS website (www.nhs.uk) only one in ten of us gets enough exercise. Some 7 per cent of heart disease deaths are related to inactivity, as compared with 19 per cent of heart disease deaths related to smoking. Evidently, we can turn the clocks back at least three years if we exercise. Many people have disabilities that mean that they can't move as much as they would like to, but most people are able to do at least some activity.

Walking is recognised as one of the best and cheapest forms of exercise; after all, all it costs is the price of some comfortable clothing and a pair of trainers. When I meet a healthy, lively older person, I usually discover that they walk several miles a day and have done for years! There are many proven benefits to walking, mental and emotional as well as physical. Walking helps to lower blood pressure and the risk of having a stroke or getting cancer, diabetes, osteoporosis or arthritis. Because it's a weight-bearing activity it can improve bone density, and because it's low impact it won't strain our joints. Walking also decreases our levels of anxiety and stress, and there are many other benefits as well. It's not as if you have to walk for hours for it to do you good. If you walk a mile in 15 minutes you will burn the same number of calories as if you had run for 8.5 minutes. One of the things I like best about walking is the thinking space it gives me. I usually try to allow my mind to freewheel and I always come back feeling as if I've been gone a lot longer than I actually have.

Now I exercise most days, but I haven't always taken such good care of myself. I was very active as a teenager and at university, and after university I even taught interpretive dance. But for most of the last decade I somehow allowed myself to get sucked into a pattern of living that didn't include time for exercise. I worked non-stop and often felt under a great amount of stress. Almost without noticing, I put on weight and became less and less fit. Then, one night four years ago, when I was still working in my office at about 11:00pm, the metal stool I was sitting on fell apart (literally, a screw came loose!) and I fell flat and hard onto a solid oak floor. Two days later I had to fly to America to see my family, so I did nothing about my back, except take painkillers. All the muscles up and down my spine seized up. Within a few months I could hardly move. I then started to take it seriously and went for physiotherapy and slowly started to exercise again and pay more attention to my health.

The fall was a wakeup call, and I realised how foolish I had been. It finally sank into my head that if I didn't take care of myself, no one else would. No one else could exercise for me, no one else could relax and rest for me, no one else could keep me well: it was up to me.

That painful and frustrating experience showed me I was not

honouring my body as part of who I was. I was not treating myself with respect. I was not treating myself as if I really believed that I was a temple of the Holy Spirit. I thought back about how hard I had been on myself, working all hours and rarely pausing for recreation of any sort. I realised with shame that if I had treated my dog the way I had been treating myself, I would probably have been reported to the RSPCA! It took a fall and a shock to my system – and months of painful physiotherapy – to transform my thinking about how I should be taking care of myself.

Now, my favourite exercise is walking, running, swimming or even going to the gym, especially if it's wet and cold outside. Sometimes when I'm doing repetitive exercise, I try to keep my mind focused only on positive things and I repeat verses or affirmations over and over as I stride along. I also try to do that when I go swimming.

I make a game of seeing if I can recite something from the Bible that relates in some way to the number of the length I'm swimming. So, for instance, if I am on length 11, I might recite inside my mind an eleventh verse that I know, such as Romans 8:11: 'If the Spirit of him who raised Jesus from the dead dwells in you, he who raised Christ Jesus from the dead will give life to your mortal bodies also through his Spirit which dwells in you.' Or if I'm on the twenty-third length, I might see how much of Psalm 23 I can remember, and so on. It's fun and helps to stave off the tedium of swimming lengths. I have to say that sometimes the moment I get into the water I am transported to some ocean or sea I have swum in, and I spend the whole time remembering either swimming over gorgeous coral reefs or riding waves. Sometimes when I want to speed up, I even pretend that I have to rescue someone from drowning. It's amazing how much faster I swim!

In addition to exercising our bodies, we can exercise our power of choice and self-control by only using words that are positive and that make us feel better. We can become more aware of how we describe things and tell stories or relate the events of the day. Our brains respond to the words we use, so when someone asks us how we are feeling, we can choose to respond by saying, 'Fine, thank you', instead of 'Not bad.' It's actually quite a challenge to try to substitute good words instead of using any negative words, even if something negative or critical has to be said.

Of course, I realise there are times when we feel intense frustration, disappointment, anger or some other negative emotion. While self-restraint is probably a good thing in most circumstances, when I am alone sometimes it feels fantastic just to let rip and bellow out exactly what I think of that unannounced detour/irritating colleague/ridiculous bit of bureaucracy – or even what I feel about a God who doesn't seem to be listening or doing anything. I expect God would rather be bellowed at than get the silent treatment!

For just one day, try not to pass on any negative stories or comments. If you have seen a tragic story in the paper or heard some awful news on the radio, do not pass it on. Edit out the sad, depressing, and outrageous things you learn about and focus instead on the good news you have heard. If you haven't heard any good news, talk instead about something that makes you feel better or happier or just talk about something you love, whether that's the colour of the sunset or the theory of anti-matter. For some reason discussing parallel universes and things like time travel and wormholes in space makes me quite ridiculously happy, as does trying to get my head around the concept of the Trinity. Also, if there's a programme about dinosaurs, or better yet, a film with dinosaurs in it, I'll be glued to the screen with a silly grin on my face. Find what works for you. Simply resist discussing the negative side of anything or anyone, just for a day. If you can do that, then try doing it for another day!

SHOPPING WELL

Those of us who are lucky enough to have access to fresh food need to be aware of what goes into producing it. We can no longer be ignorant of some of the horrors practised in the name of profit and cheap food. It is our responsibility to learn about what goes on behind the scenes in producing our food so that we can shop as responsibly as we can.

Right after leaving university my mother roomed for a time in a house with an elderly landlady who had originally come from Eastern Europe. Mother would sometimes accompany her to the shops and help carry her groceries. This lady was very particular and had high standards when it came to food. She would become quite incensed if she discovered old or tired fruit and vegetables. She would pick up a lettuce or courgette and examine it minutely.

If it did not meet her exacting standards she would throw it onto the floor in disgust, declaring loudly, 'Dead! Dead!'

Mother may have been embarrassed by this dramatic behaviour, but I have no doubt that she was influenced by it. She always took great care when shopping, and like her eccentric landlady, she would reject anything that was wilting or damaged, muttering and murmuring in exasperation about slipping standards, almost as if it pained her to see the poor vegetables in such a condition.

Of course, in many parts of the world taking this type of care is an impossible luxury. It is a case of eating what is available. For millions of people, it is a case of not having enough. One of this planet's greatest obscenities is the unequal availability and distribution of good, fresh food.

Even if a cure for all disease were to be developed tomorrow, and even if all the governments in the world were to agree on a system of food distribution that would mean no one would ever go hungry again, in the time it would take to produce enough medication and to implement the good system, hundreds and thousands more people would die. But we have to start somewhere and we have to believe that things can be different. It is not only up to the scientists, politicians, economists and aid agencies: the decisions that each and every one of us makes help – or hinder – in creating a better future.

At the very least we can consider the air miles involved in bringing particular products to us and learn about the effect their export has on the population of the country in which they were produced. If lots of air miles are essential for us to have a particular product, such as chocolate, coffee, tea or bananas, at least we can check that what we are buying is fairly traded.

> Ask, and it will be given to you; search, and you will find; knock, and the door will be opened for you.
>
> MATTHEW 7:7

FOR FURTHER THOUGHT

- What is my attitude towards taking care of my body?
- What is my attitude towards food?
- What changes do I want to make during Lent?
- Do I believe I have access to divine power?

FOR PRAYER

- Pray for people who do not have enough food to eat and who will go to bed hungry tonight.
- Pray especially for children who have never known anything other than hunger and who do not have enough food and nourishment to grow.
- Pray for all the people around the world who are involved in producing the food we eat.

FOR FURTHER READING

- Genesis 1
- Matthew 6:25–34
- Romans 8

ENTERING INTO THE SPIRIT OF LENT

Hope Not Dead

Lent has come early this year;
the muffling and damping of joy,
the empty cup, the change all spent, the train missed,
the argument, the silence.

Earlier, I washed my skin all over
and dried myself with my rough towel.
No fabric softener, no powder, no perfume.
I put on my oldest, darkest clothes,
faded, torn, stained.

And yet,
I call myself a follower of the Way,
I believe in Christ's resurrection,
I hold onto faith.
It is true:
inside my dusty boots,
shrouding my tired feet,
my socks, unseen, are golden yellow.

FORTY DAYS AND FORTY NIGHTS

The season of Lent is a time for focusing on the life and death of Jesus Christ, in preparation for the greatest Christian celebration of all – Easter. Lent is especially a time for contemplating the events of the final week of Jesus' earthly life. It is also a time for reflecting on one's own life and faith. Periods of self-reflection and self-discipline may be good in themselves, but the distinctive feature of Lent is that our soul searching is done in the light of our relationship with God.

The word 'Lent' comes from the Old English *Lencten,* meaning spring. It spans the period of forty days before Easter and is traditionally a time of fasting and penance – the practice of considering one's sins and shortcomings and expressing regret for them to God. Initially, the practice of penance first began as a public ritual, probably inspired by some of the passages in the New Testament that focused on self-discipline and good behaviour, but it developed into a more private activity within a few hundred years of the death and resurrection of Jesus Christ.

In the letter to the Romans, Paul writes: 'I appeal to you, therefore, brothers and sisters, by the mercies of God, to present your bodies as a living sacrifice, holy and acceptable to God, which is your spiritual worship. Do not be conformed to this world, but be transformed by the renewing of your minds, so that you may discern what is the will of God – what is good and acceptable and perfect' (Romans 12:1–2).

Two phrases in that passage leap out as powerful models for how we might approach Lent. The first is the phrase 'living sacrifice', which implies a willing and voluntary giving of ourselves to God, including bringing our thoughts, desires, attitudes and actions in line with what we understand to be God's will for us. It implies more than just going through the motions of an objectively worthy course of action, however good that may be. Rather, it involves bringing everything that we are into alignment with what we believe God is calling us to be, in spite of what others are doing or even in spite of all the messages from all the tired tapes of the endless *oughts* we have been told and sold in our lives.

The second phrase is 'the renewing of your minds'. This gives us the vision and hope for being able to understand more about what God may be saying to us, and it also carries with it the challenge of being able to change our point of view. We don't have to be stuck in a rut and feel we will never understand any more than we do at present. If our minds can be spiritually renewed then it is possible for us continually to change and grow – and that's good news!

There is also a passage in a letter to the Corinthians that holds a key for how we might approach Lent: 'Now the Lord is the Spirit, and where the Spirit of the Lord is, there is freedom. And we all, with unveiled faces, seeing the glory of the Lord as though reflected in a mirror, are being transformed into the same image from one degree of glory to another; for this comes from the Lord, the Spirit' (2 Corinthians 3:17–18).

It is by following the way of Christ that we discover true freedom, and knowing and living in this freedom actually makes us more like Christ. The disciplines and practices of Lent are not meant to shut us down – to make us less of who we are – but rather they are intended to open us up even more to the light and love of Jesus Christ.

LETTING GO AND TAKING ON

I think that it is most helpful if we take on new things in Lent as well as giving up certain things. The discipline of self-denial is different from the discipline of doing something new and different. Both are important and both can show us new things about ourselves and about God.

> Before they call I will answer, while they are yet speaking I will hear.
>
> ISAIAH 65:24

Things to Give Up for Lent
Procrastination
Apathy
Envy
Jealousy
Greed
Laziness
Indifference

Chocolate
Sugar
Chips
Crisps
Alcohol
Sweets
Meat
Processed food
Criticising
Negative thoughts
Cynicism
Worry
Being miserable
Holding grudges
Feelings of revenge
Feeling like a victim
Putting yourself down
Judging yourself
Judging others
Gossiping
Making excuses
Blaming others
Shopping for things you don't need

I will not fail you or forsake you.

JOSHUA 1:5

Watching TV
Listening to the radio
Reading newspapers
Going on the internet

Things to Take On during Lent

Eating healthier food
Spending less on food
Forgiving
Being positive
Thinking loving thoughts
Complimenting other people
Accepting compliments from other people
Being grateful
Being thankful
Smiling
Singing
Walking
Dancing
Volunteering your time
Giving away some money
Drinking more water
Getting up earlier
Going to bed earlier
Doing a detox
Joining a gym
Reading the Bible

Memorising a bible verse
Phoning friends and family
Visiting friends and family
Inviting friends to visit you
Being nice to neighbours
Writing letters
Making something instead of buying it
Drawing something
Sorting out your papers
Sorting out your clothes
Sorting out your other belongings
Giving away what you no longer need or use
Doing a spring clean
Standing up for what you believe in
Making time to listen to the radio
Watching TV programmes that broaden your horizons
Reading books you've been meaning to read
Cancelling subscriptions to magazines and papers you no longer read
Random acts of kindness

'I will lead the blind by a road they do not know, by paths they have not known I will guide them. I will turn the darkness before them into light, the rough places into level ground. These are the things I will do, and I will not forsake them.'

ISAIAH 42:16

> For I, the LORD your God, hold your right hand; it is I who say to you, 'Do not fear, I will help you.'
>
> ISAIAH 41:13

A SPIRITUAL EXERCISE FOR LENT

There is a sense in which each of us has to discover who Jesus is for ourselves. We are presented with certain images and descriptions of Jesus, but, ultimately, the goal is to know Jesus Christ for oneself, not to become acquainted only with what others have said about him, however true and meaningful those descriptions may have been.

Our personal quest is to discover a *person*, not just some abstract ideal. In this way each of us can talk about 'my' Jesus, not taking anything away from what others know to be 'their' Jesus, but rather adding to the body of understanding about who Jesus was, and is.

I once went on an eight-day silent retreat at St Beuno's, a centre for Ignatian Spirituality near St Asaph in North Wales. The wildness and beauty of the surroundings did much to clear out the cobwebs of my mind, as did my daily sessions in the art room. I also met daily with a spiritual director who guided me through the week, occasionally suggesting a book to read or a thought to consider. One of the books she gave me was a little volume called *The Personal Vocation* by a Jesuit named Herbert Alphonso, who is based at the Ignatian Spirituality Centre in Rome.

Alphonso tells the story of a fellow Jesuit who came to him one day saying that he could no longer pray. Alphonso asked him if he had at any time in his life ever felt spontaneously close to God. The man answered that whenever he thought about how good God had been to him, he immediately felt closer to and more in touch with God. Alphonso was inspired to suggest to this man that he should go away and not even try to pray, but that he should simply concentrate on God's goodness to him.

When the man came back, first after three weeks and then after four months, he said he found he was able to pray again when he had thought about the goodness of God. But even better than being able to pray again, the man found that thinking about God's goodness had also changed his understanding of who he was and his own calling. It had even changed his relationships and how he approached his times of relaxation and recreation. In fact, it had transformed his entire life and outlook. He discovered that over and above being a priest, he had been called to dwell on, rejoice in and pass on something of the goodness of God.

Alphonso tried this exercise himself and with other people who came to him for spiritual direction. He found that when people concentrated on the times they have felt most spontaneously close to God, they became more integrated, more alive and knew themselves to be more truly who they had been created to be.

I did this exercise and found it confirmed what I already

suspected: I feel closest to God and most like myself when I concentrate on *delighting* in God and life, and in the creatures I have been given to care for and enjoy – human and otherwise! Part of my unique personal vocation seems to be to pass on to others a sense of delight and to give them a glimpse of how God loves and delights in us. When I asked my spiritual director what she had discovered when she had done this exercise, she replied that she felt closest to God when she thought about the compassion of Christ.

'My grace is sufficient for you, for power is made perfect in weakness.'

2 CORINTHIANS 12:9

There is no fear in love, but perfect love casts out fear; for fear has to do with punishment, and whoever fears has not reached perfection in love.

1 JOHN 4:18

FOR FURTHER THOUGHT
- What is it that makes you feel spontaneously close to God?
- Have you ever been on retreat or attended a quiet day?
- How would you feel about going on a silent retreat?

A MEDITATION ON TIME

We live in time, and to a large extent, are ruled and governed by time. Yet we worship a God who is outside of time, and we know ourselves to be citizens of eternity.

Sometimes, we experience time in a linear way: we live day by day, we have a past, we exist in the present and we look ahead to the future.

At other times, we seem to live more in the past, or we are so caught up in preparing for the future that we ignore the time we are given now.

We own time in different ways, with time for family and friends, time for work, time for ourselves, and sometimes we set time aside for God.

We allow ourselves time off.

At times we call 'time out'!

Today, let us relax and rejoice in the faith that the God who knows we live in time is able to be with us all the time.

This is the God who has seen our beginnings, who understands our present existence and who knows our endings.

With this God, our endings in time signal a new stage in our eternal life, where there is no ending.

We ask our God of grace to bless this time we have now, with the peace that passes understanding, and we pray for understanding, wisdom, joy, and above all, love. Amen.

(This meditation is adapted from one I wrote in June 2000 to use when I led worship at a meeting of the Archbishops' Council.)

So I tell you, whatever you ask for in prayer, believe that you have received it, and it will be yours.

MARK 11:24

AN ALTERNATIVE APPROACH FOR WHEN IT ALL GETS TOO MUCH

Our ultimate goal is closeness to God, which we call holiness, and that is a proper goal, but sometimes we need to lighten up and just *be*. For those moments when the thought of reading another worthy Lenten meditation makes you feel like chewing the curtains, here are some fun ideas.

- Every once in a while remember to play with your food. I keep a particular photograph of my brother Joel on my wall. In the picture he has a slightly manic grin on his face and half a lemon stuck on his head. It's a good antidote when things get a bit too serious and I start losing my perspective.
- If you have young children and they're not interested in eating, make landscapes out of their food. Go for mountain scenes, lunar

I am confident of this, that the one who began a good work among you will bring it to completion by the day of Jesus Christ.

PHILIPPIANS 1:6

landscapes or underwater scenes depending on what food you're having and create dramatic narratives. Instead of nagging them to eat more, they'll have so much fun they may even take a few more bites, especially if they're eating the baddies!

- If you have middle-school age children and they are complaining about doing their homework or looking bored, as you prepare supper stick a broccoli or cauliflower floret over your ear, or even in your ear. Make fangs from celery sticks and put them in your mouth, so that when your children come into the kitchen to ask when supper will be ready they'll get a little surprise! An occasional French bean up your nose is especially good for getting the attention of unmotivated children.

- If you've got teenagers at home and they're not really engaging with you any more, announce at the dinner table one night that you are considering becoming a nudist while at home. I did this and my daughter became much more attentive, almost twitchy! The possibility will have been planted in their minds and you'll probably never even have to go through with it. I got the idea from Jack Nicholson, who let it be known he'd become a nudist at home.

- A helpful tip for being able to whizz through the weekly shop without having to stop and chat to friends and neighbours is to wear a wig. Changing your hair really changes your look. Even if someone thinks it's you, they won't be certain and they are unlikely to risk coming up to you to verify your identity. A bonus is that it's fun being incognito for a while, even if it's only in Tesco.

- When you're feeling flat, and you know you've already had your caffeine quota for the day, try telling yourself some jokes. If you're like me, you won't remember either the punch lines or how to get to them, or maybe even what the joke was about, which will instantly improve your outlook. This is also a good one for when other members of your family are feeling a bit lacklustre.

- Take up sketching and drawing. It doesn't matter what artistic talent you have. In fact, starting from a fairly low base may even help to heighten the feel-good factor. I've drawn and painted all my life, but when I'm having an off day, I find drawing insects somewhat reviving, especially if I draw them with big teeth.

- Order some personalised pens or pencils from a reliable office supplies company. If you have a responsible job, one that requires probity and sobriety, choose unusual names and slogans, such as 'Wild Coyote All Night Saloon', or 'Hedda Hotpants' or even 'I Did it with Bob'. Put some of the pens in amongst the other pens and pencils in your pencil pot on your desk. As your colleagues borrow them, as they inevitably will, enjoy hearing their reactions when they finally read the message. The real prize would be for your boss to take one of your pens into the boardroom and only spot the slogan in the middle of an important meeting with the clients. If you are the boss, have the pens distributed with the notepads for the meeting.

Do not worry about anything, but in everything by prayer
and supplication with thanksgiving let your requests be
made known to God.

PHILIPPIANS 4:6

I'm sure you can think of other things to lift your spirits. Answering
the door with a hurriedly applied avocado facemask is always a
reliable mood enhancer.

FASTING

Yet even now, says the Lord,
return to me with all your heart,
with fasting, with weeping, and with mourning:
rend your hearts and not your clothing.
Return to the Lord, your God,
for he is gracious and merciful,
slow to anger, and abounding in steadfast love.

JOEL 2:12–13

Do you not know that in a race all the runners compete, but only one receives the prize? So run that you may obtain it. Every athlete exercises self-control in all things. They do it to receive a perishable wreath, but we an imperishable. Well, I do not run aimlessly, I do not box as one beating the air; but I pommel my body and subdue it, lest after preaching to others I myself should be disqualified.

1 CORINTHIANS 9:24–27

Is not this the fast that I choose:
to loose the bonds of injustice,
to undo the thongs of the yoke,
to let the oppressed go free,
and to break every yoke?
Is it not to share your bread with the hungry,
and bring the homeless poor into your house;
when you see the naked, to cover them,
and not to hide yourself from your own kin?
Then your light shall break forth like the dawn,
and your healing shall spring up quickly;
your vindicator shall go before you,
the glory of the Lord shall be your rearguard.
Then you shall call, and the Lord will answer;
you shall cry for help, and he will say, Here I am.

ISAIAH 58:6–9

MY STORY

I came to fasting early in life. My parents were both lifelong Episcopalians, and my mother in particular was very traditional and devout, at least in how she approached her faith. Then, when I was five, my sister Robin, seven, and my brother Joel, four, my parents made a bold and life-changing decision. At the time, we were living in Huntington on Long Island. My father resigned from a job which he loved, working as a scout for Oxford University Press and driving back and forth across America, going to all the best universities and persuading lecturers and professors to write their books for OUP. My mother resigned from her job as a teacher and gave up all her community activities, including playing the violin with the local orchestra. My parents sold our car and our sweet, neat, white-painted wood-shingled home. They gave Telemachus, our adored black and white cocker spaniel, to our neighbours and moved our family onto a little wooden sailing boat.

This was not entirely out of the blue: my father had owned the boat, the *Tappan Zee*, for some time. He'd had the boat for years before he and my mother were married. My mother used to joke that she married the man and the boat, which suited her just fine. The *Tappen Zee* was a rustic but seaworthy 38-foot schooner of Dutch design with two tall slender masts, each made from a single tree. The boat became our home for most of the next ten years, except for a spell of two years when we decamped back to Long Island when my grandfather became ill and then died.

We left Huntington and sailed down the Intracoastal Waterway on the east coast of the United States and then cruised all around the Bahamas, stopping for days or weeks or even years on various little islands. We spent the last year of our time afloat as a family sailing around the Mediterranean, often following in Saint Paul's footsteps and experiencing some of the same weather conditions he encountered in his travels.

From the very beginning of our lives aboard the *Tappan Zee*, we established a daily pattern of prayer and worship. Grace was said before every meal, which we all took turns leading. At night, when the oil lamps were burning in our little cabin, or when the last light of the setting sun was still visible through our portholes, we would gather in the main cabin, with each of us children perching on either our mother's or father's bunks.

Once together we would say our prayers, each of us contributing an expression of gratitude or a request as we were moved to do so. We always ended by saying the Lord's Prayer and sometimes our mother would lead us in reciting verses from a psalm. Then, we would sing hymns until we began to fall asleep, and one by one, Robin, Joel and I would kiss our parents goodnight and go and climb into our own little bunks.

This pattern continued more or less unchanged, even when we were based for a time on a remote island and living in a cottage near where our boat was docked. In the few days before Easter when I was nine years old, my mother suddenly announced that we would all be fasting from Good Friday until Easter morning. She explained that it would show our respect to Jesus and, in a small way, help us to remember his suffering and sacrifice for us.

I have no recollection of whether my father and sister and brother also fasted, but I most certainly remember what it was like for me. I dutifully ate nothing all day Friday and Saturday, and I can remember feeling quite weak by Saturday afternoon. Usually I would spend most afternoons swimming and running and playing on the beach with my brother and sister, having completed all my lessons by lunchtime. But I can dimly remember feeling too weak and listless to play. I ached to eat something, but I did not want to disappoint Jesus, or my mother.

Early on Easter Sunday morning I woke up before anyone else and went and found a canister of raisins. I tiptoed outside to the beach and sat on the sand stuffing raisins eagerly and gratefully into my mouth while the sun rose over a calm sea. I will never forget the almost immediate feeling of energy that began to flow through me as I ate the raisins. Raisins had never – and have never – tasted so good. I felt revived as their life-giving sweetness coursed through me; within minutes my weakness and light-headedness were replaced with energy and clarity.

My mother must have noticed the effect fasting had on me and the rest of the family, or perhaps she just changed her mind about the wisdom of requiring children to fast for so long, because she never again insisted that we fast from after supper on Maundy Thursday until Easter morning. However, that was not the end of my fasting as a young person.

At the end of our time sailing, our family moved back to Long Island, this time to live in our grandparents' house in Bridgehampton. My sister Robin went away to boarding school, but Joel and I stayed at home and went to the Hampton Day School, a new school that had opened in Bridgehampton. Our family joined the congregation of St Ann's Church, the local Episcopal Church, and Joel became an acolyte. I was by then 15 and Joel 14, and like many teenagers we were constantly hungry. My mother had, however, instigated a new fasting observance on Sunday mornings, and we were not allowed to eat anything until after we had been to church and had taken Holy Communion.

Joel and I were, on the whole, obedient children, and went along with the new pattern of Sunday morning fasting. I found it difficult and tedious, and instead of taking my mind off food and inspiring me to think higher thoughts, not having breakfast before going to church only made me think more of my rumbling stomach! But apart from fantasising about hot buttered toast and other things of the flesh during the services, I was fine.

Poor Joel, though, did not take well to our Sunday morning fasting. At several of the services, which always began at 9.00am, as he stood at the side of the altar, usually surrounded by a cloud of incense, he would suddenly crumple onto the floor in a heap of white and red robes, all the colour drained from his face. This happened

He gives power to the faint, and strengthens the powerless.

ISAIAH 40:29

again and again with predictable regularity, until, finally, my mother relented and allowed us to eat breakfast before going to church.

When I was 18 I went to university in California, 3,000 miles away from home. My mother had been raised in California, and she and her sister had gone to a small independent college called Pomona College. So I set off to Pomona College, with the intention of becoming better acquainted with the West Coast and my Californian relatives.

Being a Christian at college was not easy. At times I was lonely and I often felt out of step with my peers, as I strove to be chaste and stay sober – goals shared by few of my friends. I was enormously busy, studying English literature and the performing arts. I was always writing essays, as well as performing in plays, taking voice lessons, singing in the choir, taking dance lessons and choreographing and performing in dance recitals. I was also running to keep fit and I had a part-time waitressing job in a home for retired missionaries.

At some point during the second year of my four-year course, I can remember feeling especially disappointed with myself, frustrated with what I saw as my many weaknesses. I also felt spiritually distracted, somewhat scattered. I had a deep desire to be closer to God, to understand more about how God might want me to live, to place myself as far as possible within the heart and mind of God, instead of just continuing praying, worshipping and talking and reading about God. At the same time I was rehearsing for a dance performance and I wanted to get my body in perfect trim.

Knowing nothing about the effects of long-term food deprivation, I initially thought about going on a 40-day fast, but reasoned that I would probably not be able to carry on with all my demanding activities. So I decided to fast for two weeks, thinking that would not weaken me too much, and it would be long enough to gain the spiritual benefits I longed for. Strangely, the memories of my Easter fast as a nine-year-old and the gnawing hunger of Sunday mornings at St Ann's had not put me off the idea of fasting. If anything, those experiences simply made me feel confident and comfortable with the idea of undertaking a longer fast.

So, at the age of 19, I went without food for two weeks. I drank a lot of water and I allowed myself herbal tea, sweetened with a spoonful of honey. I expect it was the honey that gave me the energy to last for so long without food. Because I went into the fast with such clear spiritual intentions, it turned out to be an extraordinary time. From about the third day I felt slightly removed from reality and I entered a calm and quiet state. Even though I still went to classes and rehearsals and greeted friends in passing, there was a new and different stillness inside me.

My detachment from food, and from all the activity that goes with shopping for and preparing as well as eating meals, seemed to create space inside me for quiet thought and constant prayer. I felt light, but not light-headed. I felt free and unencumbered: I was at peace.

I can't remember what my two roommates thought about what I was doing. All I remember is the sense of detachment, of freedom and peace. I felt closer to God. I viewed other people from a slightly different perspective and found myself listening more closely to them, saying less and just being more present with them. Having no caffeine for the entire time slowed me down somewhat, but because I was fasting, instead of feeling sluggish or lethargic, I just felt quieter. As I had been drinking several cups of coffee and tea a day, I did go through the few days of headaches that caffeine withdrawal tends to cause, but apart from that, I had no negative physical reactions for the whole fast.

> Those who wait for the LORD shall renew their strength, they shall mount up with wings like eagles, they shall run and not be weary, they shall walk and not faint.
>
> Isaiah 40:31

When the two weeks were up, and the day came when I had decided to eat again, I can remember the strange feeling as if I was somehow saying goodbye to God. It felt as if I was leaving God – leaving yet not leaving, but certainly changing the dynamics of our relationship, at least on my part. I did not want to lose the internal silence and stillness, the sense of being able to listen with keener ears, the sense of closeness. I did not want to lose the peace, but I knew it was time for me to start eating again.

I was alone when I took the first bites of my first meal, some plain cottage cheese. The next day I had a scrambled egg and some fruit and a salad. The day after that I was more or less back to normal, readjusting to the world of thinking about and eating food.

It is impossible for me to convey all that I experienced and gained during that fast, but among many other things, I discovered what it feels like to create a different type of internal space for being with God. Since then, I have fasted numerous times, but never for as long. I have realised that some of the fasts I have undertaken have not felt like proper fasts, and I did not sense any greater closeness with God or gain deeper spiritual insight either during or after the fast. If there were benefits, they were either purely physical or

Because he himself was tested by what he suffered, he is able to help those who are being tested.

HEBREWS 2:18

perhaps to do with a greater disciplining of the will, valid things in themselves, but not the main purpose of fasting.

In the Sermon on the Mount Jesus gives his followers instructions for how to fast: 'And whenever you fast, do not look dismal like the hypocrites, for they disfigure their faces so as to show others that they are fasting. Truly I tell you, they have received their reward. But when you fast, put oil on your head and wash your face, so that your fasting may be seen not by others but by your Father who is in secret; and your Father who sees in secret will reward you' (Matthew 6:16–18). Fasting is something between the one who fasts and God. It is not intended to be used to impress others with one's piety. For me, it requires above all a desire to be with God, a serious intent to listen to God without the distractions of normal life.

It is usually not necessary to fast for a long time, and this closeness and attention can come sometimes by not eating one or two meals, either inside a day or overnight. It is possible to fast even while still eating a little food, for instance, having a few apples during the day. It can even happen without giving up tea or coffee or a bowl of soup, but it cannot happen without an alignment of the spirit, heart, mind, body and will, dedicating all that is in oneself to God.

It is perhaps like inviting a dear friend into your house and then sitting quietly with your friend, listening to what your friend wishes to say to you. It is not a one-way exercise, but involves giving and receiving, listening and disclosing, being present and attentive. Although I find it easiest to fast when I can be alone, it is possible to fast while at work, going to meetings and surrounded by other people.

I have also found that fasting requires – and inspires – honesty. I become more aware of the ways in which I am comfortable with God and those in which I feel a degree of discomfort or dissonance. Is that reasoning genuine, or do I now see it revealed as being a sham? Am I really comfortable with that line of thought, or in the greater stillness do I discover the futility of my plans? Have I allowed myself to get off track or be led into a spiritual dead end? I find so many questions I never thought I needed to ask get asked, and answered, when I fast. The effect is like holding up a clear mirror or suddenly being able to see out of a window, or realising a necessary course of action, perhaps not surprising if fasting really is about drawing closer to God and listening.

Ultimately, of course, words fail to describe adequately what fasting is like, because it is like trying to describe a relationship – the halting discovery of someone else and of oneself. These things cannot even be described between two people, much less between a person and the Holy Spirit, but somehow in the simple act of a fast, there can be recognition, transformation and healing.

May those who sow in tears reap with shouts of joy.

PSALM 126:5

BEING HUNGRY AND HONOURING OUR BODIES

There are so many ways of being hungry, not just for food. There is the hunger for peace and calm, the hunger for security and safety, for sleep, rest, respite. There is the hunger for a special place or person, for the smell and sight and sound of somewhere or someone familiar and beloved. There is the hunger for touch. There is the hunger for beauty, for a certain piece of music, or for absolute silence and stillness. There is the hunger to be appreciated and recognised, seen for who you are. There is a hunger for knowledge, for something new or different. There is the hunger to be known and understood.

Sometimes it seems like too much to ask to refrain from eating because of the enforced fasting from so much else in life that one longs for. When that is the case, go easy on yourself and do not demand more than you can give. A time may come when you have the inner resources to withhold food from your body, but it is never something to be undertaken when all of life seems like sacrifice and denial.

It is recognised in many religious traditions that an empty space within the body acts like a magnet for spiritual energy. Even if we cannot or do not choose to fast, when we practise the art of mindful eating, of always leaving a little space within when we eat, then we are treating our bodies with respect. Eating moderately or fasting occasionally may seem like a denial to our bodies, but it actually represents an honouring of our bodies.

We cannot properly experience the fullness of what it means to be a human being living on planet earth unless we recognise the connectedness of our bodies with our hearts and minds and spirits. We are not merely souls and spirits inhabiting a physical body, like a hermit crab in a shell; rather, our bodies are part of who we are and shape as much as our minds and hearts of our experience and understanding of life. It has been said that our biology becomes our biography. I believe it is also true that our biography becomes our biology.

I once walked into a treatment room of a sacral-cranial therapist, to whom I had gone for help with relieving persistent headaches and a sore back. The therapist immediately announced 'There are knives sticking out of your back.' She could not offer any further insight into my situation; all she would say is what she saw. It was up to me to interpret what she had seen, but her revelations helped me to understand part of what was causing my aching head and back.

> But he knows the way that I take; when he has tested me, I shall come out like gold.
>
> JOB 23:10

FOR FURTHER THOUGHT
- For what do I hunger?
- When I think of fasting or going hungry how does that make me feel?
- Do I accept that I am body, mind and spirit?

FOR PRAYER

- Ask God to help you eat mindfully and in a way that honours your body as a Temple of the Holy Spirit.
- Pray for people who live with physical disability, pain and suffering.
- Pray for wisdom and discernment about the things in your life from which you need to fast.

FOR FURTHER READING

- Psalm 51
- Luke 4:1–21
- James 1

FOOD

Welcome dear feast of Lent!
(George Herbert, *Lent*)

FOOD FOR LENT

The season of Lent begins on Ash Wednesday, so called because of the practice of marking the foreheads of worshippers with ashes that have been blessed, a practice which has been going on for over a thousand years. The day before Ash Wednesday is also an important part of the preparation for Lent. Shrove Tuesday got its name from the word *shrove*, the past tense of the old English word *shrive*, meaning to obtain absolution for one's sins by confession and doing penance. On Shrove Tuesday it was the custom to use up all the foods you would not be eating during Lent, and so people would mix together the eggs, flour and butter they still had to make pancakes and other rich dishes. They would also celebrate with dancing and singing and dressing up in outlandish costumes. The word 'carnival' came from *carni vale*, meaning in Latin 'goodbye to meat', and the literal meaning of the celebration known as Mardi Gras is Fat Tuesday. It became the day to eat rich food and express sometimes lewd and base emotions before the sombre and sober forty days of Lent. Observation of Shrove Tuesday has been around since at least AD 1000.

It has been a tradition in the Roman Catholic Church for centuries to refrain from eating red meat on Fridays as a mark of respect to Jesus in memory of Good Friday. Instead of meat, people ate fish, a tradition still practised widely. If you don't do this already, it could become part of your Lent observance only to eat fish on Fridays. Fridays were formal fast days, and it was considered permissible to eat fish on fast days. Different dishes were prepared just for Fridays, and specifically, Fridays in Lent. In southern France, for instance, devout Catholics would eat *Brandade de Morue*, a dish made of cod mixed with mashed potato and olive oil, something which is easy enough to recreate today.

In medieval times in parts of England, whelks were eaten during Lent, boiled with vinegar and parsley. William Warham, who was once rector in the little Hertfordshire village in which I live, was enthroned as the Archbishop of Canterbury in 1504. It is recorded that at the grand dinner that followed the ceremony he served his guests a dish of sturgeon garnished with 4,000 whelks!

In the eighteenth century there were recipes for roast lamb that called for adding salted anchovies. Strong herbs were used, to remind people of the time when the Passover meal was instituted, when God spared the Israelites who ate a hastily prepared meal of unleavened bread and roast lamb cooked with bitter herbs. You can read about the story of the Passover in Exodus 12. Thousands of years later, Jesus' willingness to die on the cross was likened to the lamb killed and eaten at that first Passover, which is why lamb became a traditional Easter dish, though eaten in joy instead of fear.

The fourth Sunday of Lent is the special celebration of Mothering Sunday, which has been marked since medieval times, and honours the Virgin Mary and the 'mother' Church. When Christianity spread across Europe, Mothering Sunday replaced an earlier celebration for the Roman goddess Cybele. In the sixteenth century people would travel home to attend services at their local churches or cathedral. Later on, Mothering Sunday became the day when domestic servants would be allowed to return home to their mothers and families.

Since the earliest observances of Mothering Sunday, people have baked special cakes called Simnel cakes, believed to be named after the Latin word *simila* for fine flour. Simnel cakes are traditionally covered in marzipan and decorated with eleven marzipan balls, signifying the eleven faithful disciples. I have included a scrumptious recipe for Simnel cake given to me by Sue Jagelman, who has prepared it for her family for years (see p. 154).

We may not choose to adopt menus and dishes from the past, but we can certainly adapt the food we eat now to heighten our senses of taste and smell and our awareness of the symbolic meaning food may have. During Lent, take the time to try, if nothing else, different herbs and spices. Experiment with new tastes and use familiar tastes in different ways. Try mint, dill and tarragon in salads and soups, or as a flavouring with vegetables. I love carrots steamed with mild curry powder, courgettes steamed with a little fresh or dried tarragon or broccoli steamed with a little grated fresh ginger root. Grate the rinds of lemons and oranges and sprinkle the fragrant gratings on fish, lamb and poultry dishes, or chop a few sprigs of fresh parsley and use on meat or vegetable dishes.

It's too early for vegetables in the garden, but you may be able to find some tender dandelion leaves, which add a wonderful, slightly bitter bite to salads. Fresh, young nettles should also be appearing along lanes and footpaths. The leaves can be picked – remember to wear gloves! – and steamed as a vegetable. One spring a friend popped in unannounced and stayed for supper. I didn't have quite enough vegetables, so I ran outside and picked some nettles and served the steamed leaves with butter and salt – I called them 'Mediterranean greens'! I don't know whether our guest knew what they were, but he ate them happily enough. The water in which nettles have been steamed or boiled can also be drunk as a health-giving tea. Nettles are famed for being good for the blood and helpful in countering the symptoms of rheumatism. This is not all they are good for: evidently during the Roman occupation of Britain, soldiers would pick nettles at the end of a long march and brush and slap them against the soles of their feet. The tingling and stinging revived their aching feet.

Our concentration during Lent should not be on food as entertainment or food as a means of displaying our culinary skills, but rather as welcome and wholesome nourishment. The recipes I have chosen reflect this lack of fussiness and bravado and tend to be simple and nutritious. I have used some of my own favourites but I have relied even more on those given to me by family and friends.

Because Sundays are designated as feast days, even during Lent, I also include some recipes for slightly richer and more substantial meals and, of course, for puddings. Even though Easter is the greatest celebration of the Christian year, it is much more customary to focus on food at Christmas. Perhaps because it follows the reflective period of Lent, Easter has not typically been associated with overindulgence, except perhaps for the tradition of eating chocolate Easter eggs!

As with everything else in this book, I offer these recipes, all of them much loved and well used by those who have created them, as ideas to inspire your mind and nourish your body during Lent. If you are like me, you may follow a recipe quite precisely the first time you use it, and then make it your own by finding ways of adapting it to suit your own tastes and traditions.

> And my God will fully satisfy every need of yours according to his riches in glory in Christ Jesus.
>
> PHILIPPIANS 4:19

Breakfast

We've all heard it a million times: breakfast is the most important meal of the day, and yet I know many people who skip breakfast who would never dream of skipping lunch or supper. Some of them say it's because they're not hungry or they haven't time, or even that they would feel sick if they had to eat anything in the mornings.

Overnight, many of the systems in our bodies shut down, but it is while we sleep that our bodies renew and repair themselves. We can feel unwell and sick if we don't get enough sleep. If you can't eat in the mornings could it be because you are not sleeping enough? Except for those people who seem to get by on five or six hours a night, most of us need around eight hours of sleep. Of course we can do without that much for periods of time, but if we are getting appreciably less than that, night after night, it could be contributing to a variety of health problems, from weight gain, to poor skin, to mental health problems, as well as to feeling nauseous in the mornings.

Liven up your morning coffee or tea by sprinkling in cinnamon or grated nutmeg or using ground cloves. Grate a little orange or lemon peel and add to it to your tea instead of milk.

Lunches and Snacks during Lent

If you normally take a packed lunch to work, try using pitta bread and stuffing it with homemade hummus (see p. 149), or make a filling by mixing sardines or anchovies with cream cheese, a squeeze of fresh lemon juice and a few leaves of fresh spinach or basil. Cook lentils the night before and add to a soup or eat on their own. If you don't already own one, buy a wide-mouthed flask and take soups to work.

For snacks during Lent, replace energy bars, chocolate and biscuits with nuts or dried fruit. I love peanut butter and am quite happy to eat it on its own with just a little bit of sugarless jam. That's great when I'm at home, but much too messy to put in a packed lunch! It's better to make something like the peanut butter and molasses balls (see p. 149) freeze them the night before and pack them in a sealed container to take with you.

There is such a variety of dried fruit these days. In addition to dates, prunes, raisins and figs, you can buy dried pineapples, mangoes, papayas and bananas. Just be aware that some of these have a very high sugar content. Dried fruit was first brought to this country in the twelfth century by returning crusaders. Because dried fruit was rare and expensive, only the wealthy could afford to eat it all year round. They often ate it on fasting days in Lent.

Whatever you do, endeavour to be more thoughtful about the food you eat. Try new and different foods. Try cutting out dairy food and replacing cow's milk with soya milk. Use butter instead of margarine. If, for example you are going to make hollandaise sauce, make it with the sweetest, purest butter and savour every mouthful. You don't have to eat it again for months, but when you do, enjoy every bit of it! Whatever changes you make, make them thoughtfully and mindfully. Aim to make every mouthful count – in terms of nutrition and taste.

One of my cousins, Crystal Woodward, lives in the south of France. Crystal's partner, Georges Adrian, is from an old farming family in the area. They have fields full of cherry trees, lavender, cantaloupe melons and other crops. The last time we visited Crystal and Georges, they served us lunches of fresh tomatoes and apricots, along with a locally-made salami and a glass of rosé wine made from grapes from their own vineyards. It could not have been simpler – we didn't even use cutlery – but they were delicious and satisfying meals. Of course, during Lent it is difficult to get food quite as fresh as that, at least in England.

Crystal also told me how Georges' father described what life used to be like in the old days. She tells how people used to take a snail and eat it raw(!), and how during World War II dandelion leaves were used as food, as other salad greens and foods were scarce. Crystal also told me that a man who had lived in Siberia could remember eating raw liver, so as not to lose any vitamins, especially in the cold months. During times like these, as Crystal put it, the recipe is *endurance* – and endurance is perhaps not a bad quality to develop during Lent.

My late mother-in-law, Margaret Rees, used to tell me about how when she was a girl during World War I, she used to have to share an egg with her sister! She also told me about food rationing and how resourceful it made everyone. Even when I was living aboard my family's boat I can remember times when we ran out of fresh food. Either we were not near land, or the weather made it impossible to get to shore, or the fish weren't biting. Then my mother would have to open a tin of stew which we would have with a few invariably stale crackers. We were also rarely in a location where we could buy ice for our little ice box, so we hardly ever ate butter, milk, cheese, fresh meat or anything else that could perish. It certainly made me appreciate fresh food when we had it!

Oo - la - la !

BREAKFASTS

Churchfield Eggs Benedict

Eggs Benedict is one of my all-time favourite meals. This is perfect to have on Easter Sunday morning. For the hollandaise sauce I always use John Tovey's recipe for quick hollandaise sauce (see p. 90).

Serves 4

4–8 eggs (1–2 per person)
4–8 slices of smoked ham or smoked back or streaky bacon rashers
    (1–2 per person)
4 English muffins
butter for spreading
3oz/75g fresh spinach
1 quantity hollandaise sauce (see p. 90)

Coddle or poach the eggs and grill or fry the bacon. Halve and toast the English muffins, place them on plates and butter lightly. Lightly steam the spinach or wilt it by placing in a hot frying pan for a few minutes.

Layer on the cooked bacon or smoked ham and spinach and put the eggs on the top. Drown with hot hollandaise sauce.

John Tovey's Quick Hollandaise Sauce

This recipe comes from *Delia Smith's Complete Cookery Course* – it always works and only takes a few minutes to make. John Tovey has kindly given me permission to include his recipe in this book. Thank you, John!

Serves 4

6oz/170g butter
1 tablespoon wine vinegar
2 tablespoons lemon juice
3 large egg yolks
a pinch of salt

Put the butter into a small saucepan and allow it to melt slowly. Place the wine vinegar and lemon juice in another saucepan and bring to the boil. Meanwhile blend the egg yolks, sugar and salt in a liquidiser or food processor – then, with the motor still switched on, gradually add the hot lemon juice and vinegar.

When the butter reaches the boil, start to pour this in very slowly in a thin trickle (with the liquidiser motor running all the time) till all the butter is added and the sauce is thickened. To keep it warm, place it in a basin over some hot water till ready to serve.

Eggy Bread

This is delicious and is a particularly useful recipe if your bread is a bit stale.

Makes 1 slice

2 eggs
4fl oz/100ml milk or soya milk
1 slice of bread
butter for frying

Mix one or two eggs and the milk into a dish large enough to hold a thick slice of bread. Soak the bread in the dish and puncture with a fork so that the bread becomes saturated with the egg and milk mixture. Leave for a few minutes.

When the bread is saturated, heat the butter in a frying pan and fry the bread. Depending on how well the mixture is blended, the eggy bread will be more or less puffy.

Serve with a pinch of salt or turn it into something even more special and cover with pure maple syrup!

Old School Popovers
KERI ATAUMBI

These are perfect for breakfasts on special occasions.

Serves 4

butter for greasing the moulds
6 large eggs
2 cups milk
6 tablespoons melted butter
2 cups plain flour
1 teaspoon salt

Preheat the oven to 375°F/190°C/Gas mark 5 and generously grease a popover pan if you have one – if not, use a muffin tin. Place the pan on a large baking sheet.

Beat the eggs lightly, then add the milk and melted butter. Stir together and gradually stir in the flour and salt. Beat just until the mixture is smooth. If there are any lumps left in the mixture, strain it.

Pour the mixture into the tins almost to the top. Bake for 30 minutes and don't open the oven door. After 30 minutes, remove from the oven, cut several slits in the top of each popover and return to the oven for 5–10 minutes.

Galette

KATHY NOBLE

This is a wonderful breakfast recipe given to me by my cousin Kathy Noble. It was first made for her parents, Peter Paul and Helen Muller, by Alice Ireys, a well-known American landscape architect who worked with her father, who was an architect, on a number of projects. Alice Ireys designed, among many other things, the fragrance garden at the Brooklyn Botanic Garden in New York.

This galette has only four basic ingredients, goes together in a flash, and is spectacularly beautiful to serve.

Makes four individual or one large galette

¼ stick/30 g of butter, melted (the original recipe calls for ½ stick, but this is not necessary!)
2 eggs
½ cup milk
½ cup plain flour

Preheat the oven to 400°F/200°C/Gas mark 6. Put the melted butter in a large cast iron frying pan or a baking dish or divide it among four smaller pans or dishes. Mix the other ingredients in a bowl just until blended. Pour into the pan or dishes and bake for 20 minutes. The mixture will puff up like a giant popover, but flat in the middle, and will slip out of the pan easily.

Serve topped with sour cream and one (or more!) of the following: mixed berries, honey, brown sugar or warmed maple syrup.

John Muller's Lalapaloosa Pancakes

My grandfather loved to make these pancakes for his grandchildren. They were so big that he called them 'lalapaloosa' pancakes! They are perfect for eating on Shrove Tuesday or for any special occasion, either for breakfast or as a pudding. Because they are so much like crêpes, they can even be eaten as a main course. If possible, make the batter a few hours ahead of time, or even the day before, and leave to stand in the refrigerator. And you might want to think about making double the amount – I am always amazed at how many of these pancakes people otherwise given to moderation can eat!

Serves 4

1 cup white flour (plain or self-raising)
½ teaspoon salt
¼ teaspoon baking powder
2 eggs
2 cups milk
butter for frying

Put the flour, salt, baking powder and eggs into a mixing bowl. Mix with a fork until the mixture is a thick paste. Then mix with an electric mixer while adding the milk and continue until there are absolutely no lumps in the batter.

When ready to cook, heat a large frying pan and coat with a knob of butter. Add a ladleful of the batter and swirl it around – take care not to add too much or the pancakes will be too thick. Cook for a few seconds before flipping over with a spatula, or toss if you're feeling brave. Be prepared for the first one to come out a scrambled mess, and persevere. Re-butter the pan before cooking each pancake.

Serve with fresh lemon slices, sugar, yogurt and maple syrup and let people make up their own. Sour cream is also good.

VARIATIONS
For a really special pudding, put one scoop of vanilla ice cream in the centre of each pancake and fold over the edges. Then pour a little maple syrup on top and a little orange or cherry liqueur. Add summer fruits (thawed from frozen if no fresh fruit is available) or tinned and drained cherries. If eating the pancakes as a main course, serve with creamed spinach, sautéed mushrooms, cooked asparagus, ricotta cheese, bits of chopped ham, chicken, fish, shellfish or anything else that takes your fancy.

Emma, Gen and Huli's Fruit Compote

My young cousin Emma and her friends Gen and Huli came and stayed for a few days during their year-long cycling trip around Europe. While they were here we had fun in the kitchen creating this simple and delicious compote. It helped that, at the time, our orchard was filled with ripe apples, plums and pears!

Serves four

2 cooking or dessert apples
2 pears, fresh or tinned (in juice)
2 peaches, fresh or tinned (in juice)
8oz/225g frozen summer fruits or blackberries (thawed)
Honey or maple syrup to taste
¼ teaspoon grated nutmeg
1 teaspoon cinnamon
½ teaspoon all spice
8fl oz/225ml water

Place all the ingredients into a large pan and cover. Cook gently on medium heat until the fresh fruit is cooked through – about 40 minutes. (If you cook it for longer, the fruit will turn to mush, which may be the consistency you want.)

Serve on its own or with plain yogurt or muesli, or as a pudding, with thick double cream or custard.

VARIATIONS
The fruit can be blended after cooking for a different look and consistency, then put into tall glasses and layered with cream for an elegant red and white striped pudding! Sprinkle chopped walnuts, pecans or almonds on top to add a bit of crunch.

Bircher Muesli
ALEX REES

This is my inspiringly hyper-fit daughter's favourite standby breakfast. For those who don't like or who can't eat eggs, this filling and energy-packed muesli will see them happily from breakfast until lunch. The only trick is to remember that it has to be made the night before.

Serves one hungry person!

4oz/115g oats
1oz/25g (about 10 pieces) dried fruit e.g. raisins, dates, apricots or figs
2oz/50g (about 20 pieces) nuts (optional)
10fl oz/275ml) fruit juice
3 or 4 tablespoons plain natural live yogurt

Put the oats, dried fruit and nuts into a large bowl. Pour in enough fruit juice (apple, orange or combinations like peach and passion fruit are delicious) to cover the other ingredients. Refrigerate overnight. The oats will absorb the juice and the nuts and dried fruit will become moist and softened. In the morning, add the yogurt, stir and eat.

SOUPS

Basic soups
JENNY STANDAGE

The only reference to soup in the Bible is in Judges 6:19. Gideon asks God for a sign that God is with him. So he cooks a goat and offers the goat meat in a basket plus the broth from cooking the goat to God to help him overcome the Midianites. He realises God is with him in the form of the Angel of God as the goat meat and the broth all go up in smoke! God speaks to him, saying 'Peace – do not be afraid' and assuring him he is not going to die. So Gideon builds an altar to God and calls it 'the Lord is Peace.'

Here is a sample basic soup recipe:

Serves 4– 6

2 large onions
large knob of butter (about 1oz/25g) or 1 tablespoon olive oil for frying
4 carrots
2 potatoes
14oz tin of tomatoes
1 vegetable stock cube or 1 tablespoon vegetable stock powder
1 teaspoon salt and ¼ teaspoon pepper
1 teaspoon cumin
1 teaspoon dried coriander or several sprigs of fresh coriander, chopped
40fl oz/1 litre water

Chop the onions into thin slices and fry them lightly in a little butter or olive oil. Chop the carrots and potatoes into large chunks and place them in a pan large enough to hold the water and the vegetables. Add the lightly fried onions and sprinkle the vegetable stock powder or cubes, cumin and coriander into the mixture. Season to taste.

Bring the vegetables and spices to the boil and simmer until the vegetables are tender. When the vegetables are cooked, liquidise or mash the mixture.

VARIATIONS

You can use different combinations of vegetables and spices – for example, cumin and coriander go well with carrots, parsnips, potatoes and squash. A little nutmeg and cinnamon is lovely to add to some soups. If you are not cooking for vegetarians then you can use chicken or even fish stock instead of vegetable stock and you can add boned pieces of chicken or fish meat. After all, Gideon's soup is goat stock! To give the soup a nice hot kick in very cold weather add some paprika from Hungary and if you are feeling exotic (and not very Lenten!) then grate some fresh ginger root onto the soup.

Then there is leftovers soup. I start with chopped onions and celery tops and add any left-over vegetables – usually potatoes. To make this soup a bit more solid I often add a dried vegetable soup mix or throw in a handful of red lentils – but first check whether you have to soak them for a while before adding them to the soup!

Soupe de Sauge
CRYSTAL WOODWARD

This is a simple recipe for when you've got nearly nothing in the house but sage leaves and a bit of bread. (If you only have rubbed sage, it will be necessary to pour the sage broth through a sieve before adding the rest of the ingredients.)

Serves 2

2 pints/1.2 litres water
6 fresh sage leaves or a tablespoon of rubbed sage leaves
1fl oz/25ml olive oil
2 slices of bread
3½oz/100g gruyère cheese
a pinch of salt

My cousin Crystal sent this recipe to me from France and I pass the rest of it in her own words:

'Let the sage leaves boil in water a little. Wait a bit then put some of the water in your friend's bowl and some in yours. Add olive oil. Toast two slices of bread (and the bread can be hard, as it will soften up in the sage bouillon), and put one in each bowl. Grate a little gruyère cheese on top. Preferably add salt. Say a little prayer and enjoy!'

Butternut Squash Soup

ANGELA REES

This is one of the most satisfying soups ever – and created by my own DDD (dear darling daughter)!

Serves 4

1½lb/700g butternut squash
1oz/25g butter
1 medium onion, finely chopped
1 or 2 cloves of garlic, chopped
1 level teaspoon mild curry powder
1oz/25g plain flour
1 pint/570ml chicken or vegetable stock
1 rounded dessertspoon tomato purée
½ pint/275ml milk (or soya milk)
salt and freshly ground black pepper
a sprig of fresh parsley or fresh dill, chopped

Peel the butternut squash, discard the seeds and fibres and dice the flesh into small cubes. Melt the butter in a large (5 pint/3 litre) saucepan, add the chopped onion and garlic and cook over a low heat for about 10 minutes until the onion is translucent. Raise the heat to medium, stir in the curry powder and cook for another minute. Stir in the flour and cook for a further minute. Stir in the stock slowly, followed by the tomato purée and the diced squash.

Bring to the boil, stirring continuously, lower the heat and simmer very gently, stirring occasionally, until the squash is soft (this can take anything from 15 to 40 minutes). Liquidise the mixture and return to the saucepan, add the milk and reheat gently, seasoning with salt and freshly ground black pepper. If the soup is too thick, add a little more milk. Sprinkle the chopped fresh parsley or dill on top for a garnish.

Chicken 'Crock Pot' Soup
SUE JAGELMAN

A great way of getting even more out of your roast chicken! This is a real frugal Lenten soup.

Serves 4

1 roast chicken carcass
2 onions, chopped
2 carrots, chopped
other vegetables to taste (e.g. 1 stalk of celery, 2 parsnips, ½ swede, 6 mushrooms, 2 potatoes, 2 stalks of leeks), chopped
salt and pepper

Place the chicken carcass in the crock pot/slow cooker and add the vegetables. Cover with boiling water and cook slowly for several hours or overnight (the smell wafting through the house in the morning is great to wake up to!)

If you want a clear soup then strain the stock – if you want a thicker one, liquidise the vegetables and stock or use a hand-held blender. Adjust the thickness as appropriate (you may not need all the stock). Season to taste.

Place the chicken bones on a plate and with two forks pull away any remaining pieces of meat – you'll be surprised at how much there is. Add to the blended soup.

VARIATIONS
Any poultry works well. If you're using the leftovers from a duck then you might want to add an orange too.

Lentil and Tomato Soup
SUE JAGELMAN

Another simple and economical soup – you can double or even triple the quantities and freeze some. This is a great soup for group lunches and being thick it transports well – just dilute with boiling water on site.

Serves 4

4½oz/125g red lentils
2 tablespoons olive oil
1 large onion, chopped
1 stick celery, chopped
14oz/400g carton puréed tomatoes/passata or tin chopped tomatoes
chopped fresh parsley or fresh basil

Rinse the lentils well (soaking for half an hour helps the cooking time but is not essential).

Heat the olive oil in a saucepan and gently fry the onion and celery for 5–10 minutes. When the onions have softened add the drained lentils and mix in to coat with oil. Add the puréed tomatoes/passata to the pan. Add another carton full of water and mix in well. Alternatively use a tin of chopped tomatoes.

Simmer for about half an hour until the lentils are soft – don't add seasoning at this stage. When cooked liquidise or use a hand blender and add seasoning to taste, This will give you a thick purée suitable for freezing or diluting with boiling water to your preferred consistency to serve. Garnish with chopped parsley or basil.

Bouillabaisse

CAROL BENTON MULLER

This may be a fish soup – but what a fish soup! This is perfect for a celebration meal for those who prefer to eat fish and shellfish.

Serves 10 (if you want to cook less, just halve the quantities)

4 tablespoons olive oil
3 well-washed large leeks, chopped
3 cups chopped onion
3 cups chopped celery
4 cloves garlic, chopped
4 cups chopped firm red tomatoes
2 cups chopped fresh parsley
3 bay leaves
12 sprigs fresh thyme
1 tablespoon crumbled leaf saffron
7 cups water
1 bottle dry white wine
4lb/1.8kg of skinned and de-boned fresh white fish, cut up into serving size pieces
4 tablespoons butter
2 teaspoons plain flour
40 fresh well-scrubbed cherrystone clams (optional)
4 pints/2.5 litres fresh well-scrubbed mussels
3 lobsters weighing between 1–2lbs/450–900g each, tails removed, and cut up in three crosswise pieces; claws cracked and removed (optional)

40 large peeled and deveined shrimps/prawns
4 tablespoons anisette liqueur (Pernod or other brand)
fresh parsley, to garnish

In a large frying pan heat the olive oil and lightly toss the leeks, onions, celery and garlic until tender (do not overcook). Put them in a large heavy soup pot. Add the tomatoes, parsley, bay leaves, thyme, saffron, water and wine and simmer for 5 minutes. Add the fish, cover and simmer for 30–45 minutes, stirring occasionally. Remove the hard sprigs of thyme, making sure all the leaves are in the mixture.

In a small frying pan melt the butter and add the flour, and slowly add to the fish stock mixture, stirring gently for 5 minutes. Turn the heat off and wait at this stage until about 20 minutes before serving.

At this time bring the stock to a light boil and add the clams and mussels. After cooking at a light boil for 5 minutes, add the lobster claws, tails and the rest of the lobster flesh. Cook for another 15 minutes, add the shrimps/prawns and anisette liqueur and cook for a further 5 minutes. By this time all the clam and mussel shells should have opened. (If they have not opened, do not eat them!) Mix extremely gently.

Serve immediately, garnished with a sprig of parsley.

MAIN MEALS

Sausage and Potato Casserole

This is an easy to make and deceptively delicious casserole. It looks like a masterpiece and tastes wonderful hot or cold!

Serves 4

2 large onions
4 tablespoons butter
3lbs/1.3kg white potatoes
1½lbs/700g kielbasa or Italian garlic sausage
4 eggs
1 pint/600ml single cream
½ teaspoon salt
¼ teaspoon pepper
2oz/50g grated Swiss cheese

You will need a 9×13×2"/33x23x5cm baking dish or roasting pan.

Two hours before dinner peel and slice the onions. Cook them gently in the melted butter in a frying pan at a medium heat for 4–5 minutes until the onions are just tender, not browned. Boil the potatoes. Remove them from the pan and allow to cool. Slice the sausage into thick (about 1"/2.5cm) chunks. Grease the dish with butter. Arrange the cooked onions, sliced sausage and sliced boiled potatoes in concentric circles (see how pretty!) in the buttered dish.

Beat the eggs, cream, salt and pepper and pour the resulting mixture over the concentric circles of onions, sausage pieces and sliced potatoes. Grate the Swiss cheese and sprinkle it on top. Refrigerate the whole casserole for about 1 hour. Then preheat the oven to 375°F/190°C/Gas mark 5 and bake for 40 minutes, uncovered.

Serve with a green vegetable such as broccoli, peas or spinach or even with a salad.

Tamale Pie
CAROL BENTON MULLER

This is one of my mother's favourite recipes. I was always delighted when I knew she was making her tamale pie!

Serves 6

5oz/140g tin chilli peppers
¼ cup butter
1 cup chopped green pepper
1 large onion, chopped
3 cloves garlic, chopped
1 cup chopped celery
1lb/450g chopped lean beef (you can also use ground turkey)
7oz/240g tin tomatoes
7oz/240g tin unsweetened sweet corn

1 cup water
14oz/400g tin chopped black pitted olives
2 cups yellow corn meal
1 cup milk
1 cup olive oil
3 eggs, beaten
1 cup chopped fresh parsley
1 teaspoon paprika
salt and pepper to taste

Preheat the oven to 350°F/180°C/Gas mark 4. Wash the seeds from the chilli peppers and put aside. Lightly sauté in butter the pepper, onion, garlic, celery and meat.

Strain the juice out of the tinned tomatoes and corn into a bowl; add the water to the mixture, and soak the yellow corn meal in it for several minutes. Add the corn meal to the vegetables and meat, stirring slowly for 15 minutes. Remove from the heat. Mix together the milk, oil, and beaten eggs and add this to the vegetables and meat, stirring until mixed. Add the other ingredients and place in a large, oiled baking dish. Bake in the oven for 45–55 minutes.

Serve with a green salad.

Chris's Liver and Bacon Casserole

This is particularly satisfying in colder weather and has the benefit of being able to be made in the morning and left to cook until the evening – real, tasty comfort food!

Serves 4

2lbs/1kg pigs' liver (for preference)
1oz/25g plain flour
6 rashers of smoked back bacon
2 tablespoons olive oil
4 cloves garlic (optional)
2 onions
1 bouquet garni (optional)
1 tablespoon herbes de Provence or Italian seasoning (optional)
2 beef stock cubes
salt and black pepper
1pt/550ml water (or red wine or sweet sherry to taste)
a dash of Worcestershire sauce (optional)
vegetables (1 potato, 1 carrot, 1 parsnip, 1 turnip, 2 sticks celery, 4½oz/125g peas – to taste)

Thoroughly wash and dry the liver and toss in plain seasoned (but not salted) flour. First fry the bacon rashers in the olive oil (with crushed garlic to taste), then add and fry the onions until translucent. Take the bacon rashers out of the pan and set aside, drain the onions and place in the bottom of a pre-warmed slow cooker. Fry the liver in the remaining oil until golden brown and place on top of the onions, and place the bacon rashers on top of the liver. The bouquet garni and herbes de Provence or Italian seasoning may be added at this point.

Take the oil off the heat and add the remaining seasoned flour and the two stock cubes, salt and black pepper. Mix thoroughly into a smooth paste, ensuring all the oil is absorbed into the mixture. Add water (or red wine or sweet sherry) and bring to the boil, stirring all the while. Add the Worcestershire sauce and more salt and pepper to taste and bring to a rolling boil for 3 minutes. Pour the sauce over the liver. Add chopped raw vegetables to taste – carrots, potato, turnips, peas, etc. Cook for at least 3 hours on medium in the slow cooker, but it can be turned to low and cooked for longer.

Serve with a green vegetable like spinach or savoy cabbage (see p. 138).

Quick and Easy Stir Fry

I like meals that can be cooked in one pan, and this stir fry is about as easy and delicious as it gets. This can be made with almost any type of poultry meat or with lamb or even with only vegetables and is especially good for using up stray bits of meat or vegetables.

Serves 4

2 tablespoons olive oil

4 cloves garlic, crushed

2 onions, sliced

1lb/500g chicken, turkey or lamb pieces (optional), cut into 1"/2.5cm pieces
   or strips

10–12 prunes

12 cashews

Between 1–2lbs/450g–900g assorted vegetables (e.g. broccoli, courgettes,
mushrooms, peppers, peas, tinned corn (unsweetened), tinned tomatoes,
water chestnuts, bamboo shoots, etc.)

7oz/200g fresh spinach

A few slices of apple (optional)

Put the olive oil in a heated frying pan and lightly brown the crushed
garlic and sliced onions. Add the pieces of poultry or meat and cook
for a few minutes, stirring occasionally.

Add the prunes and cashews, broccoli, courgettes, mushrooms,
peppers, peas, tinned corn, perhaps some tinned tomatoes, or try
some tinned water chestnuts or bamboo shoots, then cover with a
layer of fresh spinach. Simmer until it reduces somewhat. Sometimes
I add a few slices of apple, especially if the apple is looking a bit tired.

Serve on its own or with rice or wild rice. You can also add some
kidney beans or chickpeas to the stir fry, if you need to make it
stretch further.

Chicken with Mustard and Lemon Sauce
PEGGY CARR

This recipe, given to me by one of my wonderful twin cousins, has a surprisingly subtle and sophisticated flavour, in spite of being so quick and easy!

Serves 2

2 tablespoons plain flour
¼ teaspoon garlic salt
¼ teaspoon onion salt
1 whole chicken breast, into 1"/2.5cm cubes
1 tablespoon (or more) butter
6oz/175g fresh mushrooms, sliced
1 chicken stock cube
1 cup water
1 teaspoon dried mustard
1 tablespoon lemon juice
½ teaspoon sugar
2 teaspoons cornstarch
1 tablespoon water

You will need a frying pan with a tight fitting lid.

Mix the flour, garlic salt and onion salt together and toss the chicken cubes in the mixture. Sauté the chicken pieces in butter in the frying pan until golden. Add the sliced mushrooms and sauté for 2–3 minutes with more butter, if needed.

Add the stock cube and the cup of water. Cover and simmer for 20 minutes. Meanwhile, in a small bowl combine the mustard, lemon juice, sugar, cornstarch, and 1 tablespoon water. Stir until blended. Add to the chicken, stir and simmer for about another 10–15 minutes until smooth and bubbly.

Serve on white or saffron rice.

Robin Muller Perez's Salmon with Orange and Ginger

This is a brilliant recipe and works well with salmon or trout. It is a wonderful combination of tastes and extremely simple.

Serves 4

1 orange
3½oz/100g fresh ginger root (more or less to taste)
1¾lb–2lb/800g–1kg fillet of salmon or trout (approx 7oz/200g per person)
1 tablespoon olive oil (optional)
1 onion (optional)
a pinch of dried herbs, e.g. oregano, marjoram, thyme (optional)
1 tablespoon maple syrup or 1 teaspoon Demerara sugar (optional)

Slice the whole orange into thin slices, leaving the peel on (cut across the orange so that the slices show the segments like the spokes of a wheel). Remove the skin from the ginger and grate it roughly.

Take a piece of baking foil large enough to make a parcel around the entire fish.

If desired, first put a little olive oil on the foil, then slice an onion thinly and place that on the foil. Sprinkle herbs such as oregano, marjoram or thyme on the onion and lay the fish on the bed of onion and herbs. Place the orange segments and grated ginger all over the top of the fish. For a lovely hint of sweetness, pour about a tablespoon of pure maple syrup or sprinkle a teaspoon of Demerara sugar on top of the orange and ginger before sealing the fish in the foil parcel.

Fold the edges of the foil together on top of the fish like a parcel. Bake the in oven at 375ºF/190ºC/Gas mark 5 for 45 minutes or steam for 30–40 minutes, checking to see if it is cooked through.

Serve with steamed leeks, courgettes, broccoli or broad beans and rice or boiled potatoes, or even freshly mashed potatoes.

Cuban Shrimps/Prawns
CUPTAL JOHNSON

This recipe for an easy, tasty shrimp or prawn stir fry was given to me by a friend at university. It satisfied me as a hungry student – and still does now!

Serves 2

2 tablespoons olive oil
1 large onion, sliced
4 cloves of garlic, minced
½ medium green pepper, thinly sliced
14oz/400 g shrimps/prawns
¾–1 cup tomato purée
1 teaspoon salt, to taste
3 pimientos, thinly sliced (optional)
a pinch of pepper
¼ cup vinegar or lemon juice
2 cups of cooked mixed vegetables, e.g. diced carrots, sweetcorn, green beans, peas, diced potatoes (optional)

Heat a pan and put a little oil in it. Cook the onions until they are translucent and add the rest of the ingredients. Bring to a boil and simmer for 20 minutes.

Serve over rice.

Grilled Fish with Devilled Cheese
KATHY NOBLE

My twin cousins Kathy and Peggy are brilliant cooks. This is one of Kathy's favourites that she kindly passed on to me!

Serves 4–6

2lbs/900g white fish fillets
butter, melted
4oz/115g cheddar cheese
2 tablespoons chilli sauce
2 tablespoons Dijon mustard
½ teaspoon horseradish sauce

Arrange the fillets in a foil-lined pan and brush with the melted butter. Grill for 8 minutes until lightly browned and flake with a fork. Grate the cheese, mix with the chilli sauce, mustard and horseradish sauce and spread over the fish. Grill for 3 minutes until melted and lightly browned.

Serve with green vegetables or a salad.

Prawn and Coconut Curry

JEAN LONGDIN

This is a fragrant light curry that is easy and quick to make. It works equally well as a lunch dish served in balti bowls with warm crusty bread or as a dinner for friends served with basmati rice and a couple of side dishes. The sauce part can be made in advance, giving the cook more time to entertain guests!

Serves 4

For the sauce
1½ tablespoons olive oil
1 large onion, chopped
½ teaspoon sea salt
½ teaspoon ground turmeric
½ teaspoon ground fenugreek
1 teaspoon ground cardamom
1 tablespoon ground coriander
½ teaspoon hot chilli powder or 1 teaspoon dried chilli flakes or 1 red chilli, deseeded and finely chopped
14oz/400g tin chopped tomatoes
½ block (approx 3½oz/100g) creamed coconut

To finish
1 bunch coriander leaves, chopped (reserve some whole for garnish)
1lb 2oz/500g (or more depending on appetite) frozen cooked prawns, defrosted overnight in the fridge and drained thoroughly on kitchen towel.

1 green chilli, deseeded and finely chopped (optional)
2 firm tomatoes, sliced thinly (optional)
1 lemon, cut into wedges

Heat the oil in a large saucepan and gently fry the onion until soft and transparent (but not brown), stirring occasionally. Mix the salt and spices together then add to onion and fry for about 1 minute, stirring to prevent sticking. Add the chopped tomatoes, mixing thoroughly. Bring to a gentle bubbling simmer, cover and cook for 20–30 minutes. If you're using uncooked prawns, add them to the sauce for the last 5 minutes of the simmering stage.

Take the pan off the heat and crumble in the creamed coconut. Stir, cover and leave to stand until the coconut has melted into the sauce, then stir again. (The sauce will look very thick at this point but don't be tempted to add any extra liquid as the prawns release moisture when heated through and the sauce will 'come right' in the end.)

In the meantime, if you're serving the curry with basmati rice, cook the rice according to the packet instructions. You could either fork the chopped coriander leaves into the cooked rice when fluffing it or stir the leaves into the curry before serving. Keep the rice warm in the oven.

Spoon the well-drained prawns into the sauce, cover and heat through *very* gently, being careful not to let it boil as this will harden the prawns.

Serve garnished with chopped green chilli and a few coriander leaves, with the sliced tomato and lemon wedges on the side.

Granny's Creamy Fish Pie
MARGARET REES

My mother in law, Margaret Rees, was a great help to me when our daughters were little. She would often come over and help out with the cooking, gardening and mending. One of the most popular dishes that she cooked was this fish pie. Even though she has now passed away, we still cook Granny's fish pie – true comfort food!

Serves 4

1lb/450g mixed fish such as cod, haddock and salmon
1½oz/40g butter
1oz/25g plain flour
½ pint/250ml milk
2 tablespoons chopped fresh parsley
salt and pepper
1lb/450g mashed potatoes

Preheat the oven to 375°F/190°C/Gas mark 5. Put the fish in a roasting tin and bake in the oven for about 10–12 minutes until opaque and starting to flake. When the fish is cool enough to handle, take off the skin, remove any bones and flake the fish into large chunks.

Make a traditional roux or white sauce by melting the butter in a pan, mixing in the flour and then gradually adding the milk, whisking gently to avoid lumps forming. Add the parsley and seasoning. Place the flaked fish in an ovenproof dish and pour the sauce over it. Mix together lightly and cover with mashed potatoes. Dot with a little butter and heat in a moderate oven for about 20 minutes.

Serve with peas and mashed or boiled potatoes.

Roasted Butternut Squash and Halloumi Pasta
ANGELA REES

I am proud to say that both my daughters have grown into excellent cooks. They are much better than I am with many things, especially with baking and recipes requiring several stages. This is one of my elder daughter Angela's best!

Serves 4

1 small butternut squash
6 shallots
12 cherry tomatoes
a handful fresh sage
1 tablespoon olive oil
7oz/200g dried pasta, shape of choice
8oz/225g halloumi
2 tablespoons pesto (see p. 123)
a pinch of salt and pepper

Preheat the oven to 350⁰/180⁰C/Gas mark 4. Peel the squash, cut in half length-ways and de-seed, then cut the flesh into approx 1"/2.5cm cubes (try to keep the size of the pieces consistent so they cook equally). Peel and halve the shallots and arrange in a pre-oiled or non-stick baking tray along with the squash and whole tomatoes. Roughly tear the sage and sprinkle over the top, add a drizzle of olive oil and season generously. Roast for 45 minutes until the squash is soft and tender.

In the meantime, cook the pasta according to the packet instructions, taking care not to over-cook it. Slice the halloumi length-ways into ¼"/½cm thick slices and grill or griddle until golden brown. (Timing is everything here, so that the pasta, halloumi and vegetables are ready at the same time).

Drain the pasta, stir in the pesto and roasted vegetables and serve in pasta bowls. Finish with slices of halloumi.

Home-made Pesto
ANGELA REES

Serves 2

2oz/50g fresh basil leaves
1 clove garlic, crushed
2oz/50g pine nuts, lightly toasted
2oz/50g Parmesan cheese, finely grated
2 tablespoons olive oil
salt and pepper

Simply blend ingredients together into a paste, adding more olive oil if required.

Rigatoni with Cauliflower and other delicious tidbits
KERI ATAUMBI

My family seems to be blessed with fabulous cooks, and my sister-in-law Keri is one of the best! She and my brother Joel live in the desert outside of Santa Fe, where they grow many of their own vegetables, including hot chillis! Santa Fe is renowned for delicious food and Keri's recipes always transport me back to that gorgeous part of the world.

Serves 4

2 teaspoons salt
1 small cauliflower, cored and separated in small florets
4 tablespoons olive oil
1 large onion, diced
¼ cup pine nuts
3 garlic cloves, chopped
2 large bay leaves
1 pinch/½ teaspoon saffron
1 teaspoon hot red pepper flakes
3 tablespoons tomato paste
½ cup raisins
½ cup water
2 cups dry white wine
12oz/350g rigatoni
¼ cup finely chopped fresh parsley
salt and pepper
Parmesan cheese, grated (optional)

Fill a large saucepan with water, add the salt and bring to the boil. Add the cauliflower and blanch for 2 minutes. Remove the cauliflower and bring the water back to the boil for the pasta.

Warm the oil in a large, heavy frying pan over a medium heat. Add the onion and a pinch of salt. Cook for 5 minutes, then add the pine nuts, garlic, bay leaf, saffron and red pepper flakes and cook for 2 minutes. Stir in the tomato paste, raisins, water and wine. Raise the heat and bring the sauce to a boil. Reduce the heat to low, add the cauliflower and simmer covered for 15 minutes.

Cook the pasta in the cauliflower water. Drain it and add it to the saucepan. Add the parsley and salt and pepper to taste.

Serve with the grated Parmesan cheese sprinkled over.

Rainbow Stew
JENNY STANDAGE

Jenny Standage and I have been friends and colleagues for many years. One of the things I have always admired about Jenny is her ability to get stuck in with any task – whether it's leading a choir, producing a newsletter or cooking for an unexpected houseful of hungry friends and family!

Serves 4

3½oz/100g black-eyed beans/peas, pre-soaked
3oz/75g yellow lentils, pre-soaked
1 vegetable stock cube
3 tablespoons olive oil
1 tablespoon dried oregano
2 onions, sliced
5 cloves garlic, sliced
8oz/225g each of potatoes, carrots and turnips, diced
1 head of celery

2 firm cooking apples
10fl oz/300ml orange juice
seasoning to taste
chopped fresh parsley to garnish

Drain the beans, then bring to the boil in plenty of fresh water, add the lentils and stock cube and simmer for 1 hour or until the beans are tender. Meanwhile heat the olive oil in a large saucepan and add the oregano, onions, garlic and the rest of the vegetables. Add a little water, stir over a low heat and simmer for 10 minutes.

Add the pulses in their stock, stir thoroughly and simmer for another 10 minutes. Slice and core the apples. Pour the orange juice into the stew and add the apples. Simmer for another 5 minutes. Season to taste and serve sprinkled with parsley.

The Guru's Quiche
JENNY STANDAGE

This is recommended as a good thing to eat before a session of prayer and meditation. It is very satisfying and filling. It also has the advantage that all the ingredients except the eggs will keep for a long time, so if you are snowed in and cannot get to the shops but you keep chickens, you can still make the Guru's quiche!

Serves 6

2 cups brown flour
1 cup sunflower oil
2 tablespoons milk
a pinch of salt
14oz/400g tin evaporated milk or 14fl oz/400ml ordinary milk if preferred
14oz/400g tin asparagus spears
4 eggs
4oz/115g grated cheese
salt and pepper

You will need a large 12"/30cm ceramic quiche dish. Preheat the oven to 325ºF/170ºC/ Gas mark 3.

Mix the flour, oil, milk and salt in the dish itself. Stir with a spoon and press to the sides to completely cover the bottom and go up the sides a little way. Use your hands to get an even base. Bake in the oven for 15 minutes.

Meanwhile take the evaporated milk and whip it up in a large bowl. Open the tin of asparagus, pour off half the asparagus liquid into the evaporated milk and whip again. Add the eggs, whipping in one at a time. Spread the cheese over the base and arrange the asparagus spears like spokes. Pour the egg mixture over the top and sprinkle with salt and pepper. Bake for 30 minutes until set (test with a knife or skewer and when this comes out clean, the quiche is ready).

Greek Spinach Pie
ALICE BALDWIN

This recipe was given to me by my friend Alice Baldwin when she heard that I was planning on getting married!

Serves 6

Approx 11–14oz/300–400g ready-made filo or shortcrust pastry
1 large onion, chopped
3 tablespoons butter
1 tablespoon dried basil
1 tablespoon dried oregano
a pinch of salt and pepper
3 eggs
1 cup cottage cheese
14oz/400g tin spinach or 1lb/450g fresh spinach

You will need an 8"inch/20cm quiche or flan tin.

Preheat the oven to 400°F/200°C/Gas mark 6. Roll out the pastry and line the pie tin.

In a frying pan sauté the onion in the butter with the basil, oregano, salt and pepper. Meanwhile beat together the eggs, cottage cheese and spinach. Add the cooked onion and herbs, mix well and turn the mixture into the pie dish. Cover with a top crust, crimp edges and slit the top.

Bake for 30 minutes until the crust is golden. Cool slightly before serving.

Robin's Quiche
ROBIN MULLER PEREZ

My sister Robin makes the best quiches I have ever had! She uses a variety of vegetables, including asparagus, broccoli and spinach, and also many different types of meat and cheese. Use your imagination (and leftovers!)

Serves 4

For the pastry
1 cup whole wheat flour
¼ cup peanut oil
¼ cup cold water
1 teaspoon salt

for the filling
¾ cup grated cheese
1 small onion, sliced
½ pint/275ml double cream or evaporated milk
3 or 4 eggs
mushrooms, sliced
green or red pepper, sliced

Preheat the oven to 350ºF/180ºC/Gas mark 4. Mix the pastry ingredients together using your hands. Roll out the dough and press it onto the pie plate. Prick the dough with a fork in several places to let steam escape before placing in the oven. Bake the pastry shell for 7–10 minutes.

Place the grated cheese in the pastry shell, add the diced onions and pour on the egg and milk mixture. Lastly, decorate with the mushrooms and green or red peppers. Bake for 45 minutes until firm and golden.

Raw Lasagne
GENEVIEVE SPELLMAN

When Gen and her friends were visiting me while they rested from their cycling, Gen told me about how she had eaten nothing but raw food for a year and a half. She gave me this recipe for lasagne that has persuaded me it is possible for raw food to be both delicious and satisfying!

Serves 2

2 courgettes
2 tomatoes
6 sun-dried tomatoes (optional)
2 cups spinach leaves
6 fresh basil leaves

For the cashew nut cheese
1 cup soaked and drained cashew nuts
juice of 1 lemon
pinch of salt
1 tablespoon nutritional yeast

For the basil pesto
4oz/115g pine nuts or walnuts
2 cups fresh basil leaves
2 or 3 tablespoons olive oil
pinch of salt and pepper
1 or 2 garlic cloves

Soak the cashew nuts for 2–5 hours and drain them, then blend them with the rest of the ingredients for the cashew nut cheese until light and fluffy (this should take about 3 minutes).

Blend the basil pesto ingredients until chunky or smooth, depending on how you like it.

Cut the courgettes into thin slices to act as the 'pasta' in the lasagne. Into a serving dish or small cake tin, layer thin slices of fresh and dried tomatoes, spinach and chopped basil, pesto and cashew nut cheese between the layers of courgettes. Cover with baking paper, clingfilm or a piece of muslin cloth and place a heavy object, such as a rock or metal weight or brick on top. Place in the refrigerator for 2–4 hours, then serve.

SALADS AND SIDE DISHES

Quinoa Salad
KERI ATAUMBI

A beautiful and unusual salad – and very healthy! Arame is a kelp seaweed often used in Japanese cooking. It is full of vitamins and minerals, including calcium, iodine, iron, magnesium and vitamin A as well as other nutrients, and is usually sold in a dried form.

Serves 2

2 cups toasted pumpkin seeds
½ cup arame
½ teaspoon salt
1 cup quinoa
1 red onion, diced
11oz/300g sweetcorn
1 red pepper, diced
1–2 bunches red radishes, trimmed and cut into matchsticks
1 large carrot, grated
2 cups sesame seeds
2 cups sunflower seeds

For the marinade
½ cup cider vinegar
2 cups olive oil
1 bunch coriander, chopped

2 spring onions sliced
1 jalapeño pepper, minced
1 garlic clove, crushed
salt and pepper

Toast the pumpkin seeds in a cast iron pan on the hob, or on a baking tray in the oven, then allow to cool. You can use ready-toasted seeds if you can find them.

Soak the arame in hot water for a few minutes. Cook the quinoa according to the packet instructions and then spread it out on a sheet of waxed paper or foil to cool.

Steam the red onion for 3 minutes and then rinse in ice-cold water to make it sweet and crisp.

Mix together the marinade ingredients, then combine all the other ingredients with the marinade and mix well. Refrigerate for about 20 minutes for the flavours to marry.

Serve with some rustic bread and cold meats or sardines if you wish.

Simple Bean Salad
KERI ATAUMBI

These beans are stupidly simple to cook, and the broth from preparing them is delicious too. The salad is a yummy and ridiculously beautiful concoction with the dark green kale, yellow squash and white or red beans looking very pretty. If you don't have time to soak the beans overnight, you can use tinned beans in the salad instead.

Serves 4

For the beans
1lb/450g dry white Italian cannellini beans
3½ pints/2 litres water
1 or 2 tablespoons olive oil
1 large head of garlic (slice the top off to expose the cloves, but don't peel or separate it)
¼ teaspoon whole peppercorns
1 very large sprig of fresh sage
salt to taste

For the salad
2 medium acorn or butternut squash
1 tablespoon olive oil
2 tablespoons balsamic vinegar
1 tablespoon honey
1 bunch kale

450g cooked cannellini beans or 450g tinned cannellini or red beans
½ onion or 1 shallot
1 large garlic clove
1 tablespoon red wine or red wine vinegar
1 teaspoon salt

First soak the dry white cannellini beans in the water overnight. Then put the mixture in a crock pot or over a low flame, add the oil, garlic, peppercorns and sage and cook the beans according to the instructions on the packet. After they are cooked add salt to taste and drain the beans, retaining the broth separately.

Preheat the oven to 400ºF/200ºC/Gas mark 6. Peel and cut the squashes into ½"/1cm thick semicircles. Toss with 1 teaspoon olive oil and spread on a parchment-lined baking sheet. Bake for about 15 minutes until tender. Mix the balsamic vinegar and honey together and brush on the squash. Set the rest of the vinegar and honey mixture aside and put the squash back in the oven for 5 minutes.

Wash and chop the kale and put it in a large bowl with the beans and the cooked squash. Heat the remaining oil in a small saucepan. Add the onion or shallot and garlic and cook until slightly softened. Add the red wine or red wine vinegar and remaining vinegar and honey mixture and bring to the boil. Immediately pour the hot dressing over the kale, toss and cover so the kale wilts slightly.

Serve on its own or with some roast lamb or other meat. Save the broth for the next day.

Quinoa Pilaf
BARBARA LUDLOW

This is a simple and satisfying dish that goes with all kinds of meat or is lovely on its own.

Serves 4

1 cup quinoa
¾ cup water
1 onion, chopped
3 cloves garlic, chopped
1 tablespoon olive oil
1 sweet potato, chopped
1 red pepper, chopped
1 cup chopped fresh spinach or kale
2 teaspoons ground cumin
2 teaspoons ground coriander
salt and pepper
½ cup chopped fresh coriander

Put the quinoa and water in an uncovered saucepan and cook it on medium heat until the quinoa has absorbed nearly all the water. Then remove it from the heat and set aside to cool.

Sauté the onion and garlic in a hot frying pan with the olive oil, then add the sweet potato and red pepper. Cook until tender. At the last minute, toss in the chopped fresh spinach or kale, cooking until just wilted, along with the ground cumin, coriander and salt and pepper to taste. Add the fresh coriander and serve. Serve with bread and cheese or meat – or on its own!

VARIATION

Many types of vegetables are nice in this dish. You can use sautéed corn kernels or courgettes, whatever is available. You could also toss in raw vegetables such as chopped cucumbers and baby fennel.

Savoy Cabbage

Chris first developed this method of cooking cabbage in order to make it more interesting than just boiling or steaming it. Now I cook cabbage this way all the time – it works wonderfully with all types of cabbage!

Serves 4–6, depending on the size of the cabbage

1 savoy cabbage
butter for frying
white pepper

Cut the cabbage into portion-size chunks or slice it fairly fine. Steam it for less than five minutes, until nearly, but not quite, tender. Make sure you remove it from the heat while it is still somewhat crunchy.

Heat a large frying pan and melt a large knob of butter in it. Sprinkle the hot butter with white pepper. Toss in the cabbage and stir for a further five minutes or so, until it is a bit crispy and brown around the edges.

Serve with mint sauce or rose or lavender jelly.

Carol Benton Muller's Stuffing
(AS APPROVED OF BY DELIA SMITH)

This is my mother's stuffing and is my all-time favourite. It can be used to stuff turkey and chicken or eaten on its own. Although I always serve this at Thanksgiving, it is wonderful to have at other times of the year too. If you leave out the giblets and cook the stuffing in a separate pan, it is entirely suitable for vegetarians.

My mother's stuffing was given the seal of approval by none other than Delia Smith! Years ago, when Chris was a producer with the BBC, he invited some of his media friends to have Thanksgiving at our house. They included Gerald Priestland and his wife Sylvia, Os and Jenny Guinness, and Delia Smith and her husband Michael. I was not daunted because I knew I was on home ground with a Thanksgiving meal! After the meal Delia asked me for the recipe for the stuffing. I think that says all you need to know about how good it is!

Serves 8
a medium loaf of sliced white bread
1 large onion
2 sticks of celery

1 apple

about 20 large black pitted olives to taste (use colossal or Graber, not the
    little pickled ones)

14oz/400g tin artichoke hearts

salt and pepper

¼ teaspoon paprika

½ teaspoon dried sage

½ teaspoon dried parsley

½ teaspoon dried oregano

12 cashews, walnuts or pecans (optional)

11oz/300g sweet chestnuts (optional)

giblets from turkey (optional)

3½oz/100g unsalted butter

Preheat the oven to 400°F/200°C/Gas mark 6. Cut the crusts off the
bread and dice the bread slices into bite-sized pieces. Place on a
baking tray one layer at a time and brown in the oven. This only
takes a few minutes, so watch them carefully. This will have to be
done in several batches in order to crisp all the bread.

When all the diced pieces of bread have been crisped, put them
into a very large mixing bowl. Cut the onion, celery and apple into
bite-sized pieces and add to the bowl. Cut the olives and artichoke
hearts into halves and add to the bowl. Add the salt, pepper, paprika,
sage, parsley and oregano, and the cashews, sweet chestnuts and
giblets (if using).

Melt the butter in a small pan. When the butter is melted pour
it all over the oven-crisp bread pieces and the other ingredients. Add
about 1 pint/600ml just-boiled water. Mix in well with a sturdy fork

(I do it with my hands when the water has cooled after a minute or two), but don't overdo it. The stuffing mixture should be moist, but not too mushy.

Stuff the turkey or chicken and roast as normal, or if cooking separately place the stuffing mixture into a baking tin, cover the stuffing with foil and put it in the oven 45 minutes before the roast will be cooked. Take off the foil for the last few minutes in order to brown the top.

Simple Orange Sauce for Roast Duck or Ham

This is a simple sauce that will transform a roast and give it that *je ne sais quois*!

Makes just over ½ pint/300ml

juice of 2 oranges and rind of 1 orange, chopped into small pieces
water (enough to make up the juice to ½ pint)
2oz/50g sugar or honey
1oz/25g cornflour

Put all the ingredients in a small saucepan and gently bring to the boil, then boil for a minute or two. Pour over the roast or serve in a little jug on the table.

Leon Wambsganss' Marinade

This recipe was given to me by a friend from Texas, who, when introduced to Guinness, immediately added it to his marinade! I use it over any kind of meat – it works well with steak, lamb and chicken. Occasionally I have been known to add a generous splash of sweet sherry when there is no stout in the house or if I want an extra bit of sweetness.

Makes 1 pint/600ml

3 fl oz/100ml olive oil
6 cloves garlic
juice from 1 lemon
juice from 1 orange
16fl oz/450ml Guinness
a large dash of Worcester sauce
6oz/200g tomato purée
a large pinch of coarse sea salt

Place all the ingredients into a bowl large enough to accommodate whatever it is that you want to marinate. Submerge the meat in the marinade, cover and leave to stand or place in the fridge. Leave for a few hours or overnight, if possible, then barbeque, grill or fry the meat as normal.

SNACKS

Walnut Chips – Just Like Crisps (only better!)
KERI ATAUMBI

Just like crisps, it's hard not to eat a lot of these, but they are full of nutrients, so you can feel virtuous as you enjoy them!

Serves 4

¼ cup walnut pieces
2 tablespoons and ½ teaspoon salt
8oz/225g green beans
3 cloves garlic, chopped
3 tablespoons olive oil
2 tablespoons chicken broth
1 cup chopped fresh parsley

Toast the walnuts. Boil 2 pints/1.2 litres of water with 2 tablespoons salt. Prepare a large bowl of iced water. Blanch the beans in the boiled salt water for 1 minute, remove, then plunge them into the ice water. When completely cool, drain and set aside.

Sauté the garlic in 1 tablespoon olive oil until lightly browned. Lower the heat, add the chicken broth and simmer for 2–3 minutes until most of the stock has evaporated.

Purée the remaining 2 tablespoons of olive oil, parsley, toasted walnuts, sautéed garlic, salt and any remaining stock in a blender.

Add the pesto to the beans and toss until completely coated. This is best served at room temperature and is great as a pick me up!

Cinnamon Toast

This is one of the most comforting snacks I know and is a great treat on a cold grey day. It can be made in just a little more time than it takes to toast a slice of bread! It's particularly good with a cup of tea or coffee or hot chocolate.

Serves 1

1 slice bread
unsalted butter for spreading
1 teaspoon caster or granulated sugar
¼ teaspoon ground cinnamon

Lightly toast a slice of bread. Butter the toast immediately. Mix together the sugar and ground cinnamon in a little cup and sprinkle all over the toast.

My Dip

This is my favourite fail-safe dip and can be made in a few minutes. I serve it with raw vegetables, (e.g. cucumber, celery, broccoli, cauliflower, peppers and carrots), or with breadsticks, crisps, crackers or little pitta breads.

Serves 6

11oz/300g cream cheese
11oz/300g mayonnaise
11oz/300g plain natural no fat yogurt, preferably set
a pinch of salt
1 tablespoon mild curry powder
½ teaspoon paprika
½ teaspoon Italian herbs
Worcester sauce (optional)
a pinch of dried tarragon (optional)
a pinch of dried dill (optional)

Place the cream cheese, mayonnaise and yogurt in a large mixing bowl. Add the rest of the ingredients. Mix well with a sturdy fork until blended together.

You can adjust the relative proportions of the cream cheese, yogurt and mayonnaise depending on how you prefer it. If you wish to cut a few calories, use reduced fat cream cheese and mayonnaise.

Hummus
AAQIL AHMED

Once when I met with Aaqil to discuss something to do with broadcasting (Aaqil is the Commissioning Editor, Religion and Head of Religion and Ethics at the BBC), I learned that he is also a dab hand in the kitchen. We started talking about favourite recipes and Aaqil kindly shared with me two dips he makes.

Serves 4

1 14oz/400g tin chickpeas
2 tablespoons tahina
1 clove garlic
juice from 1 lemon
pinch of salt and pepper
1 tablespoon olive oil
paprika (optional)
pomegranate seeds, separated (optional)

Drain the chickpeas and put them in a blender. Add the tahina, garlic, a good glug of lemon juice and salt and pepper to taste. Blend all the ingredients and taste. If the hummus is too dry add a little water. If the tahina taste is too over-powering add more lemon juice. Serve with a generous topping of olive oil and either a sprinkling of paprika or a handful of separated pomegranate seeds. Eat with pitta bread.

Baba Ganoush
AAQIL AHMED

Use the hummus recipe and replace the chickpeas with one large oven-cooked aubergine. Bake the aubergine whole in the oven at 400°F/200°C/Gas mark 6 for about 30–40 minutes. You will know it is ready when the natural oils start to ooze out and the skin is all shrivelled. Allow the aubergine to cool and then take off the skin before blending the flesh with the rest of the hummus ingredients.

Stilton Dip

This is a ridiculously quick and simple recipe and absolutely delicious!

Serves 4–6

4oz/100g Stilton cheese
2½fl oz/75ml fresh double cream or 5oz/150g cream cheese
5oz/150g natural yogurt
2 teaspoons chopped fresh parsley
salt and pepper

Mash the Stilton until soft. Lightly whip the cream or cream cheese and mix with the Stilton, Stir in the yogurt and parsley. Season to taste and mix well. Place in a bowl and chill before serving. Serve with crackers or celery.

Peanut Butter and Molasses Balls

This was one of my favourite snacks as a teenager. It is high in energy and good for instant energy on the go. This is particularly easy for children to make. My daughters used to have great fun making all sorts of wiggly shapes out of the mixture.

Makes a 12 balls the size of large marbles, or a few large peanut butter slugs!

7oz/200g peanut butter (with no added sugar or salt)
1–2 tablespoons dark molasses
1 tablespoon powdered milk (optional)
Demerara sugar (optional)

Mix the peanut butter with the molasses and the powdered milk. Adjust the amounts depending on how much of the mixture you want to make up and whether you prefer more or less molasses. If you do not have powdered milk or you do not want to use it, that's fine, just make sure the consistency of the mixture is firm enough to hold a shape.

Take a small lump of the mixture and roll it into a ball between the palms of your hands. Do the same with the rest of the mixture. For added crunch and sweetness, roll the balls in a little Demerara sugar.

Place in a plastic container and freeze for about an hour. Take the balls out as and when you want them. They only need a few minutes to thaw before they are ready to eat and they travel particularly well for energy on the go. You can also store them in the refrigerator if you prefer them less hard.

PUDDINGS

Churchfield Mess

This is my version of Eton Mess. Use whatever soft fruit you can get, whether it's fresh, tinned or thawed from frozen. Strawberries, raspberries, blueberries or a summer fruits combination are all delicious, and tinned peaches or cherries are also good.

Serves 6–8

6–8 shop-bought meringue nests
14oz/400g Chantilly cream or double cream
¼ teaspoon vanilla essence (optional)
1lb 2oz–1¾lbs/500–800g fresh, tinned or frozen soft fruit

Lightly crush the meringues into large pieces in a mixing bowl. Mix in the Chantilly cream or double cream. If you are using double cream add the vanilla essence to the mixture. Then lightly mix the fruit into the meringues. Chill before serving, or eat straight away!

If you like gilding the lily, this can also be served on top of a little ice cream or sorbet.

Plum Crostini with Thai Chilli

KERI ATAUMBI

This has an intense, delicious flavour.

Serves 4–6

¼ cup plain flour
1½ teaspoons salt
½ teaspoon sugar
4oz/115g unsalted butter
2 tablespoons iced water
1½ cups port
1¼ cups brown sugar
1 or 2 Thai chillis
2lbs/900g small Italian plums, halved and pitted
¼ cup cornstarch
¼ teaspoon cinnamon
1 teaspoon double cream
sugar for dusting

You will need an 8"/20cm torte pan. (You can also use a pie pan or quiche dish.)

Blend the flour, ½ teaspoon of salt and ½ teaspoon of sugar in a mixer or food processor. Add the butter and blend until the mixture is a coarse meal. Slowly add the iced water until it just sticks together. Tip out on to a piece of cling film and form into a circle. Wrap the dough in the clingfilm and refrigerate for 30 minutes.

After 30 minutes, roll out the dough on a lightly floured surface and line the torte pan with it. The dough is really crumbly, so I just fill in the tears with bits of dough. Don't touch it or roll it too much as it may get tough. Freeze for 30 minutes.

Preheat the oven to 400°F/200°C/Gas mark 6. Simmer the port, ½ cup of brown sugar and the chillies in a saucepan until the sauce is reduced to ½ cup.

Stir together the remaining brown sugar and remaining salt, plums, cornstarch, cinnamon and port syrup. Transfer to the torte shell. You can brush what crust there is with the cream and dust with sugar.

Place a piece of foil on the oven shelf below the one the torte will sit on, since it spits and boils a little. Put the torte in the oven and bake for 30 minutes, then reduce the oven temperature to 375°F/190°C/Gas mark 5 and bake for a further 1½ hours until done.

Serve the torte with vanilla ice cream with a few chunks of crystallised ginger chopped up and stirred into it.

Bishop's Cake
KERI ATAUMBI

This is a delicious, moist and foolproof cake.

Serves 4–6

8oz/225g butter
2 cups sugar
2 cups plain flour
1 tablespoon lemon extract
1 teaspoon vanilla extract
2½ tablespoons almond extract
5 eggs

Preheat the oven to 350ºF/180ºC/Gas mark 4. Heavily butter and flour a bundt pan (a deep cake tin with a hole in the middle). Cream the butter and sugar. Add the flour, lemon extract, vanilla extract and 1 tablespoon of the almond extract and mix well. Beat in the eggs one at a time.

Bake for 30 minutes uncovered, cover with foil and bake for a further 30 minutes, then uncover and bake for a further 15 minutes. Remove from the oven, turn out the cake onto a large plate and drizzle the remaining almond extract over the top while it is hot.

Let the cake cool and serve with ice cream and berries and a couple of toasted almond slivers if desired.

Simnel Cake
SUE JAGELMAN

This seems like a long and complicated recipe, and it certainly involves a lot of ingredients, but it is worth it to achieve this scrumptious cake!

4oz/100g natural coloured glacé cherries
2oz/50g chopped mixed peel
9oz/250g currants
100g/4oz sultanas
zest of 1 lemon
8oz/225g plain flour
good ½ teaspoon of cinnamon
½ teaspoon freshly grated nutmeg
pinch of salt
6oz/175g butter (at room temperature)
6oz/175g caster sugar (golden unrefined if available)
3 eggs (at room temperature)
1 tablespoon brandy or milk if required

For decorating
1lb 2oz/500g block of ready-made yellow marzipan
icing sugar
apricot jam or smooth marmalade for spreading
mini chocolate eggs

Line the bottom and sides of a deep round baking tin (mine is 7½"/19cm but a bit smaller or larger won't matter.) Preheat the oven to 300°F/150°C/Gas mark 2. I use a non-fan oven for cakes so you may need to reduce the temperature a little for a fan oven.

Lift the cherries out of any sticky syrup and chop into halves or quarters. Mix the fruit together in a bowl, and grate the lemon zest into the bowl too.

Measure out the flour and sift into another bowl, adding the spices and salt. Cream the soft butter with the sugar in a mixing bowl using a hand-held electric whisk. Break the eggs into a measuring jug and whisk slightly with a fork to blend.

Add the eggs to the creamed butter and sugar *a very small amount at a time*, whisking on high speed to incorporate into the mixture. If you add too much too fast it will curdle, so patience is required! If it does begin to curdle a small amount of flour can be added to stabilise the mixture. Gently fold in the flour and then the fruit mixture using a metal spoon. The cake mixture needs to drop fairly easily off the spoon – add the brandy or milk if required.

Fill the cake tin with the mixture and level the top, making a slight depression in the central area (this helps the final cake surface to remain flatter when rising during cooking, and makes decorating it easier). Cook in the centre of the oven for about 2½ hrs until golden brown on top and firm to the touch.

Remove the cake from oven and leave to cool in the tin for an hour or so before turning it out and removing the lining paper. When completely cool, wrap in greaseproof paper and store in a cake tin until ready to decorate.

DECORATING THE CAKE

Mould about two-thirds of the marzipan into a ball. Dust a pastry board and rolling pin with icing sugar and roll out the marzipan into a circle to fit the top of the cake (use a piece of string or a ruler to help you measure).

Brush the top of the cake with melted apricot jam or smooth (not chunky) marmalade. Place the marzipan on the cake and smooth down. Roll pieces of the remaining marzipan into 11 small balls (representing the 11 faithful disciples) and arrange around the edge of the cake, fixing to the marzipan covering with jam/marmalade.

Make a little nest out of the rest of the marzipan and place it in the centre of the cake. Fill with mini eggs. In our family the nest 'miraculously' refills with eggs each time the cake appears and a fluffy chick has been known to perch on the nest too!

Easter Chocolate Cheesecake
SUE JAGELMAN

This cheesecake is so rich and scrumptious that it should only be eaten on high days and holidays! The quantities for the chocolate topping aren't critical – if you use a larger amount of cream cheese you may want a bit more chocolate and cream. The difference is really in the thickness of the topping in the tin.

Serves 8

For the base
8oz/225g digestive biscuits
2oz/50g butter
1 tablespoon Demerara sugar (not essential but gives extra crunch)

For the chocolate topping
9oz/200g cream cheese (low fat is fine, but full fat tastes even better!)
3oz/75g caster sugar
2 large eggs
5fl oz/150ml double cream
5oz/150g bar dark chocolate with a high cocoa content

You will need a springform 9"/23cm cheesecake tin, greased with butter. Get the cream cheese and eggs out of the fridge in advance as they mix/beat more easily at room temperature.

To make the base, break up the biscuits, place them in a

polythene bag and bash into crumbs. Melt the butter in a large pan, then add the biscuit crumbs and sugar, if using. Spread the mixture over the base of the tin, firm down well and place the tin in the refrigerator.

To make the chocolate topping, put the cream cheese in a mixing bowl, add the sugar and blend well. Separate the eggs, add the yolks to the cream cheese mixture and retain the whites to beat. Whip the double cream until thickened but not solid!

Break the chocolate into pieces in a bowl and melt, either over a pan of hot water or in the microwave – don't overheat it! Beat the egg whites until firm. Add the melted chocolate to the cream cheese mixture and blend. (At this stage you need to work fairly quickly as the chocolate may be starting to set.) Fold in the whipped cream, then fold in the beaten egg whites using a metal spoon until just blended. Pour the chocolate topping onto the biscuit base and refrigerate until set.

To serve, decorate the cheesecake with candy-coated mini chocolate eggs at regular intervals around the circumference. This keeps well in the fridge if you can manage to restrain yourself and anyone else in the house from eating it immediately!

Grilled Bananas

These are simple and always delicious. They also make a perfect pudding for unexpected guests, as there are usually a few bananas in the fruit bowl!

Serves 4

4 bananas
unsalted butter
2 tablespoons maple syrup
2 tablespoons Demerara sugar
½ teaspoon ground nutmeg
¼ cup rum (optional)
vanilla ice cream (optional)

Peel the bananas and cut in half lengthwise. Place the bananas on foil under a hot grill with a tiny knob of butter on each half. Pour a small amount of maple syrup over the banana halves and sprinkle with a little brown sugar and ground nutmeg. Grill until the banana halves are bubbly and going slightly brown. Then, if desired, put the rum in a small saucepan and warm through until the rum is hot, but not boiling. Do not allow the rum to boil.

Place the bananas on plates and pour the rum over them. Light with a match and carry to the table while the rum is burning, or place on the table first, taking care to stand back! When the flames die, place a scoop of vanilla ice cream on top of each banana or just enjoy the bananas on their own.

Granny Hall's Cheesecake
SARAH SMITH

In the 1960s Mary Farrow gave this recipe to Betty Hall, who passed it down to her daughter (and my friend!) Sarah Smith. I have enjoyed this cheesecake for nearly three decades and can vouch for its utter deliciousness!

For the base
3oz/75g unsalted butter
6oz/175g biscuits (50% Nice and 50% digestive, or you can use only digestive biscuits), crushed
2oz/50g caster sugar

For the middle
1lb/450g full fat cream cheese (low fat doesn't work – what a pity!)
3 medium sized eggs
5oz/150g caster sugar
1 teaspoon vanilla essence
1½ teaspoons lemon juice

For the topping
14fl oz/400 ml soured cream
1½oz/40g caster sugar
½ teaspoon vanilla essence

You will need a 9"/23cm non-stick loose-bottomed cake tin.
Preheat the oven to 350ºF/180ºC/Gas mark 4.

To make the base, melt the butter in a saucepan and blend in the crushed biscuits and sugar. Spread the mixture over the base of the tin and firm down well.

To make the middle section, blend the cream cheese, eggs, caster sugar, vanilla essence and lemon juice well in a large mixing bowl. A hand-held electric beater helps! Pour the mixture over the base. Cook for approximately half an hour until it is set. (Don't worry if the top cracks a bit because it gets covered up!) Remove from oven and leave for 5 minutes.

For the topping, mix the cream, sugar and vanilla essence well and carefully spoon the mixture over the top of the cheesecake. Place back into the oven for at least 10 minutes. Remove from the oven and allow to cool. Decorate with white grapes cut in half and placed around the circumference of the cake – or with anything you like!

Canadian Butter Tarts
MYRNA GRANT

This recipe has been handed down in a family from Nova Scotia and is over 100 years old. I was not given the recipe for the tart shells, so I have adapted a recipe for plain pastry. This pastry is sweeter and is especially good for open pies and fruit tarts.

Makes 6–8 tarts depending on size of individual tarts

For the pastry
8oz/225g plain flour
½ teaspoon salt
1 tablespoon sugar
6oz/120g butter
1 egg yolk
1 tablespoon cold water
1½ tablespoons lemon juice

For the filling
½ cup raisins or currants
1 beaten egg
¼ cup butter (melted)
½ cup brown sugar
¼ teaspoon salt
1 teaspoon vanilla
½ cup corn or maple syrup or 1 additional cup brown sugar

Preheat the oven to 400°F/200°C/Gas mark 6. You will need a well-greased 6–8 hole muffin tin.

Mix the flour, salt and sugar with the butter and egg yolk using a blender, two knives or even your hands. Sprinkle the water and lemon juice on the mixture, stirring it in with a fork until you can pat the pastry lightly into a ball and then, touching it as little as possible, roll out the pastry, cut out into circles and place into the muffin tin.

For the filling, pour the hot water over the raisins. Drain. Add the butter and all other ingredients. Pour into the unbaked tart shells and bake for 15–20 minutes.

Apple Crumble

Crumbles may be modest creations, but they are also some of the most simple and delicious puddings and they are very satisfying! A traditional crumble is made from cooking apples, but I use whatever fruit is in season, or that I have in tins or in the freezer. As an alternative to apples I use plums, pears, blackberries, strawberries, cherries, quinces and bananas. Sometimes I also add a few raisins, dates or even a few pieces of fresh orange.

Serves 4

2lbs/1kg (roughly 4–6) cooking apples, or the equivalent amount of other
    fruit
2oz/75g Demerara or brown sugar
½ teaspoon cinnamon
½ teaspoon all spice
6oz/200g self-raising flour (plain flour also works)
3oz/100g unsalted butter

Preheat the oven to 375°F/190°C/Gas mark 5.

Peel the apples (you do not have to remove absolutely all of the peel) and cut into large bite-sized slices. Put them in the dish you will be cooking them in – I always use a deep glass baking dish so that I can see when the fruit has cooked. Sprinkle half the sugar, the cinnamon and all spice on the fruit.

To make the crumble, put the flour and the other half of the sugar into a large mixing bowl. Cut the butter into thin chunks (if I remember, I take the butter out of the fridge at least half an hour before I need it). With your hands, mix the butter into the flour and sugar until you can squeeze it lightly into large clumps. Add a little more butter if the mixture is not clumping. Put the crumble on top of the fruit and bake for 30–40 minutes, depending on how quickly the fruit cooks.

Serve with vanilla ice cream or hot custard.

Carrot-Oatmeal Biscuits
MICHELLE DESAULT

The recipe for these delicious biscuits was given to me by a childhood friend. The biscuits are perfect to make on a rainy weekend afternoon and eat curled up with a good book or watching an old film.

Makes 5 dozen

2 cups whole wheat flour
1 teaspoon baking powder
¼ teaspoon baking soda
½ teaspoon salt
¼ teaspoon nutmeg
¼ teaspoon cinnamon
1 cup rolled oats
1 cup raisins

½ cup butter or a light vegetable oil
1 cup brown sugar
2 eggs, beaten
2fl oz/75ml milk
1½ cups grated raw carrots

Preheat the oven to 350°F/180°C/Gas mark 4. Sift the flour with the baking powder and baking soda and add the salt and spices. Add the rolled oats and raisins.

In a separate bowl, cream the butter or oil and sugar and add the eggs, milk and carrots; then add this to the first mixture. Mix well. Drop by teaspoon onto a greased baking sheet. Bake for 15 minutes and allow to cool for a few minutes before eating.

Bavarian Cream Coffee
MRS TISDALE

This is extremely delicious recipe was given to me when I was a teenager by a very elderly and quite grand lady. Her daughter, Nancy, was in her forties and had Down's Syndrome. I used to come to their house several afternoons a week to play games with Nancy. She was fiendishly good at draughts and canasta and not bad at chess, although I remember that the pieces would occasionally make some rather creative moves!

Serves 2

¼ cup cold water
1 sachet of gelatine
2 cups sugar
¼ teaspoon salt
½ cup very strong instant coffee
2 cups cream, whipped
1 tablespoons lemon juice
1 packet of sponge fingers

Pour the cold water in a bowl and sprinkle the gelatine on top. Stir. Add the sugar, salt, and coffee and stir until dissolved. Cool and when the mixture begins to thicken, beat and fold in the whipped cream and lemon juice. Turn into a bowl lined with sponge fingers.

Lemon Snow

This was one of my mother's favourite recipes. I can remember my delight whenever she made it.

Serves 6

1 envelope unflavoured gelatin
¾ cup sugar
a pinch of salt
¾ cup boiling water
1 teaspoon grated lemon peel
¼ cup lemon juice
3 egg whites

Mix the gelatin in ½ cup cold water. Add ½ cup of sugar, the boiling water, a pinch of salt and stir. Add the lemon peel and lemon juice. Refrigerate until the consistency is like unbeaten egg whites, for approximately one hour. Beat the egg whites until foamy and gradually add the remaining sugar. Beat until soft peaks form when the beater is raised. Beat the gelatin mixture until foamy and then mix the gelatin mixture into the egg whites. Put the combined foam mixture into a bowl large enough to hold it. Refrigerate until firm.

If possible, serve in shallow champagne glasses or in any stemmed dessert dishes, then add a layer of the Pouring Custard on top. For decoration, sprinkle a little grated lemon rind on the top of the individual glasses.

Pouring Custard

12 fl oz/450ml milk
3 egg yolks
¼ cup sugar
dash salt
½ teaspoon vanilla essence

Heat some water in a saucepan to simmering point and place a heatproof bowl or another saucepan on top. Put the milk in the bowl or top saucepan and heat until tiny bubbles appear around the edge of the milk. Put the egg yolks, sugar and salt into a bowl and mix well. Very slowly, pour the hot milk into the egg mixture, beating constantly. Now pour the mixture into the heatproof bowl or top saucepan and replace it on top of the saucepan with the simmering water. Stir constantly for 8–10 minutes and test with a metal spoon – the custard is done when it forms a thin coating on the spoon. Pour the custard immediately into a bowl and cover with waxed paper. Set the bowl in cold water to help it cool. Stir in the vanilla essence and refrigerate. Serve on top of the 'snow' or separately in a little jug.

Olga Popoff's Pascha

This traditional Russian Easter dessert has been passed down through generations of my father's family. When my grandmother, Olga Popoff Muller died, my mother carried on making her mother-in-law's pascha at Easter. When I married and moved to England, I brought the recipe with me and have made it nearly every year. I love knowing that other members of my extended family also still make Grandmama's pascha.

Serves 8

1 egg
½ cup sugar
*2lbs/900g cottage cheese
*1 14oz/400g packet cream cheese
*½ pint/275ml sour cream
(* if you prefer a creamier and denser texture, use less cottage cheese and
      more cream cheese and sour cream)
½ cup chopped blanched almonds
½ cup raisins and candied lemon and orange peel
¼ teaspoon almond essence
¼ teaspoon citron essence
¼ teaspoon vanilla essence
¼ teaspoon lemon essence

To decorate
blanched almonds
raisins

Mix the ingredients in the order given until creamy. Put the mixture into a large sieve lined with a clean piece of muslin cloth. Tie the ends of the cloth over the top and place a plate on top. On top of the plate place a heavy object, like a half a brick, an iron doorstop or a glass paperweight. Keep in the refrigerator overnight.

To serve, turn upside down onto a large plate and decorate with some extra raisins and blanched almonds. On one side spell out in raisins 'X B', which stands for Christ is Risen. On the other side make a Russian Orthodox cross in raisins. For more decoration, make lines of raisins and almonds going from the top to the bottom of the pascha. On the very top place a freshly-cut red rose.

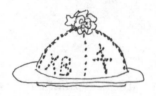

COOK'S NOTES

I buy my olive oil in bulk from Elanthy, imported from Greece by the Straight Forward Trading Company. It is cold pressed and extra virgin. Their website is: http://www.elanthy.com or call them on Freephone 0800 169 6252.

REFLECTIONS
FOR HOLY WEEK
AND EASTER

Faith is the assurance of things hoped for, the conviction of things not seen.

HEBREWS 11:1

'For nothing will be impossible with God.'

LUKE 1:37

Again Jesus spoke to them, saying, 'I am the light of the world. Whoever follows me will never walk in darkness but will have the light of life.'

JOHN 8:12

'Everyone who lives and believes in me will never die.'

JOHN 11:26

We know that all things work together for good; for those who love God, who are called according to his purpose.

ROMANS 8:28

But Jesus looked at them and said, 'For people it is impossible, but for God all things are possible.'

MATTHEW 19:26

MAUNDY THURSDAY

Maundy Thursday is the day on which Jesus and some of his closest friends shared their last supper together. It is also the day on which Jesus was betrayed by Judas, one of his disciples. The Last Supper became the template for Holy Communion, the blessing, giving and receiving of the bread and the wine, one of the Christian sacraments.

It was also on Maundy Thursday, before they ate supper, that Jesus washed his disciples' feet. On this day many Christian churches and house groups hold a ceremony of foot-washing and I can testify what a moving ceremony that can be. Years ago when I was at a simple foot-washing service in the home of a friend, I was inspired to wash my uncle's feet. No sooner had I begun, when suddenly, it was as if his feet became Jesus' feet and I felt as if I was kneeling in front of Jesus while he let me wash his feet. I cannot describe the love I experienced, from my uncle, but also somehow from Jesus. Since then, other foot-washing services have been moving and meaningful, but I have never again had that conviction that I was actually holding and washing the feet of Jesus, while he looked down on me with infinite and tender love.

I have been asked to preach a number of times on Maundy Thursday, and I offer the following as a reflection for this day, when Jesus enters the final twenty-four hours of his earthly life.

Maundy Thursday reflection

In our thoughts we can attempt to enter into the great darkness and despair of Jesus' betrayal and subsequent death, and try to stay with those events, tonight, tomorrow and Saturday, before allowing ourselves to emerge into the dazzling brilliance and radiant joy of Easter.

Quite rightly, the tragic and dreadful events of Good Friday obscure the dimly lit and muffled hours in the Garden the night before. The stark, awful horror of nailing a living human being to a piece of wood, the bloodthirsty crowds, the brutish soldiers ('Just following orders, Gov'), the grieving friends (those who had not already run away), the ebbing, broken, torn life, the desolation of Jesus on the cross, the agonising death, the apparent finality and hopelessness – these are the images which haunt us, which demand our full attention.

But it was on the night before, after Jesus and his friends had eaten supper together, when they had gone out to the Garden to pray, that the events of Good Friday were actually determined and set in motion.

Jesus still faced the physical pain of his death and the emotional anguish of seeing his mother and closest friends in their grief and despair – but it was on the night before, in the Garden, that he accepted the final act of his mission and committed himself to going through with whatever lay ahead.

That night he prayed, sweating blood and crying out loud, so agonising it was for him to accept what he knew was to come – saying to God, 'Yes, I will do this. If this can be taken away, please take it away, but, nevertheless, not my will, but yours.' What faith, what obedience, what submission to the divine will, to the God he knew intimately as Abba – but still, the sweating blood.

How much does Jesus' faithfulness cast our difficult decisions into perspective? How much does the setting of his will to see through the events of this life-and-death-changing-week put our vacillating, weak and selfish wills to shame? What a gulf there seems to be between us and Jesus, between me and Jesus.

It is almost too painful to imagine how I would have acted. Yes, Jesus, I would have stayed awake! I would have prayed with you! I would have stuck with you, even after you were arrested. I wouldn't have denied you!

T. S. Eliot once reflected that it is our sickness which is our only hope; our sin is in fact our salvation, because it is our sickness, our disease which brings us back, time and again, to God, to the sight of Jesus hanging on the cross, where we can see both the cost of our sin and the depth of God's love.

How can we ever get away from the betrayal – the many and repeated betrayals – the cruelty, the inhumanity, the fear and the cold concern for ourselves, at times above all others?

How do we not let this night of failure – this tragic fiasco – paralyse us for ever? What are we supposed to think about Judas, what are we supposed to think about the chief priests and Pharisees, what are we supposed to think about Peter and the other disciples? What are we supposed to think about ourselves, when we wonder what we would have done? Would we really have found ourselves with Mary Magdalene and Jesus' mother and John at the foot of the cross, or would we have been long gone, huddled and snivelling in some safe hideaway?

The events of the night in the Garden are some of the most sobering events of the entire Gospel story. They shame us, anger us, distress us, grieve us, but they are perhaps too easy to imagine, too easy to reconstruct in the mind's eye, with our knowledge of human nature and our knowledge of ourselves. What if Eliot is right? What if our sickness is our only hope? What if our disease is actually the way to our health?

What if it is only by forcing ourselves to face Gethsemane, to place ourselves there among Jesus' friends that night – eager, willing, loyal, confused, terrified – that we can come to understand more of the cost of our sin and more of the depth of God's love?

Tonight, we can hardly look Jesus in the face. We want to hide from what happened in the Garden. We want to pretend it wasn't the way it was, that Jesus' friends, and Jesus himself, only did what they had to do, that they could not have done otherwise, that they each had their roles to play, that they were just sticking to their scripts.

But that would be to deny the free will that God has given us, and to deny that Jesus had free will, even then. We would like to think that if we had been Jesus' friends we would have stayed awake, prayed with him, supported him, defended him. But we know we would have betrayed Jesus. Even if we wouldn't have betrayed him then, we have all betrayed him in one way or another now, by not standing up for him, by not trusting in him, not keeping faith with him.

In order to move out of the Garden, as we will need to do in a few days' time, not only in our heads and hearts, but in our lives, we need to forgive what went on in the Garden. We need to accept what happened, as Jesus accepted, as the Father accepted. We need to forgive Judas, for being the man he was and for doing what he did. We need to forgive Peter and the other disciples who deserted Jesus. Perhaps we even need to forgive Jesus, for asking so much of his friends, for asking so much of us, for having been perfect where we would have failed.

We also need to forgive ourselves – for our imperfection, our weakness, our humanness, our 'sickness', our sin. We need to learn to accept what we are and who we are. We need to accept that God loves us, just as we are, and that Jesus chose to die for us, knowing exactly what we are like. We need to remember that, in spite of the Garden, in spite of Good Friday, in spite of all the horrors that we have ever done and will ever do, we have been made in God's image and the Spirit of the Divine dwells in each and every one of us.

We need to forgive ourselves for doubting God's capability, God's commitment to us, God's faithfulness to us. We need to forgive ourselves for resisting God's enduring, transforming love, which is the greatest power there is.

We need to see that it is this love that is the only way out of the Garden, the only way through Good Friday, the only Way. We need to understand that it is the power of this love that made the first Easter possible, and that this love is still here, still with us, still waiting to transform our lives, if we let it.

Taken from a sermon preached at St Mary Magdalen Church,
Barkway, Hertfordshire on Maundy Thursday, 9 April 2009

FOR FURTHER THOUGHT

Picture the events of Maundy Thursday: the foot washing, the last supper, Jesus' arrest in the Garden of Gethsemane and Peter's denial.

- What do you relate to most?
- How do you think you would have behaved if you had been one of Jesus' close disciples?

FOR PRAYER

- Pray for all Christians who are persecuted for their faith.
- Pray for increasing unity and harmony among the different Christian churches.
- Pray for the strength and courage to be faithful to Christ in all the circumstances of your life.

FOR FURTHER READING

- Matthew 26:17–75
- Mark 14:12–72
- Luke 22
- John 13—18:27

GOOD FRIDAY

Can we think about our focal symbol, the cross of Jesus, and try to rescue it from its frequent fate as the banner of our own wounded righteousness? If Jesus is indeed what God communicates to us, God's language for us, his cross is always both ours and not ours; not a magnified sign of our own suffering, but the mark of God's work in and through the deepest vulnerability; not a martyr's triumphant achievement, but something that is there for all human sufferers because it belongs to no human cause.

ROWAN WILLIAMS, *Writing in the Dust*

We preach Christ crucified ... to those who are called, both Jews and Greeks, Christ the power of God and the wisdom of God. For what seems to be God's foolishness is wiser than human wisdom, and what seems to be God's weakness is stronger than human strength.

1 CORINTHIANS 1:23–25

Put away from you all bitterness and wrath and anger and wrangling and slander, together with all malice, and be kind to one another, tender-hearted, forgiving one another, as God in Christ has forgiven you.

EPHESIANS 4:32

Then Jesus said, Father, forgive them; for they do not know what they are doing.

LUKE 23:34

Entering into Good Friday

It is a sad and aweful thing to contemplate what Jesus went through on the day he died. Apart from the fact of his innocence and the sheer injustice of it all, the raw emotion, physical pain and degradation is almost too much to bear.

But it is important that we enter into Good Friday for many reasons. We cannot get away from the fact of death; Jesus' death, our own death, and the death of every single other living human and creature on planet earth. Knowing that one day we will die, we can ask ourselves, how do we want to live?

I have occasionally met people who seem to prefer Good Friday to Easter morning. They are stuck in pain and suffering. I've been there myself. My mother died in the summer of 2009, and when Good Friday came the next year, it felt only marginally worse than what life had been feeling like for the past eight months. I had been thinking about death and grieving for my mother every day for all that time and Good Friday just seemed to be part and parcel of that process.

I didn't really pay much attention to Lent and I certainly didn't think about giving up anything that year, because it already felt as if I'd given up all that mattered. I remember by the time Good Friday came, I hadn't done anything to prepare for Easter. Then something lovely happened. Two young girls in my village came up to visit me. I cannot remember why or what was on their minds, but I suddenly realised I hadn't even put together my Easter egg tree, something I do every year. I asked them if they would help me to prepare it and they agreed, not knowing, of course, how grateful I was to them for taking on this seemingly simple and lovely task.

So the girls and I walked along one of the footpaths in our village, and found a suitable branch for the tree. We brought it home and I secured the branch in a sturdy vase so that it would not twist or fall over, and gave the girls my collection of little painted wooden eggs on strings and left them to it. They did a beautiful job.

I may have had my Easter egg tree, but that year I could not really face the symbols of new life. There was still too much pain. But, in spite of my grief, Easter came two days later, as it always does. As many people have observed, the saddest and the gladdest days for Christians are only two days apart!

Saying Sorry

Good Friday is partly about facing our own mortality, our complicity with the sin and suffering of the world and our own individual culpability. It is about saying we are sorry for all the bad we have done and all the good we have left undone; it is about facing up to our own subtle, or not so subtle, wiliness, pettiness and peevishness. As we know, there are people in this world who have committed unspeakable acts of cruelty and wickedness. Most of us, thank God, never have and never will, but we are not without sin. Each of us is responsible for what we think and what we say and what we do, and collectively we are responsible for creating a just and caring world.

Part of our Lenten duty and discipline is to admit and acknowledge our sins, whether they are sins of omission or commission, but, for some reason, saying sorry – apologising – is really difficult. We are perfectly happy to say 'sorry' many times every day when, in fact, we more properly mean 'excuse me'. When travelling in a crowded tube train I always hear a chorus of 'sorrys' around me, which is as it should be. It is good to be courteous and thoughtful to others, and acknowledge when one has stepped on someone else's feet or inadvertently elbowed someone, but that is on a very different level from saying sorry to God or to the people we have really hurt.

It is at this deeper level that saying sorry suddenly becomes the 'hardest word', as the song goes. And yet, to sustain any long-term relationship, whether it is with our work colleagues or with our closest family and friends, it is absolutely essential to apologise for the things we inevitably do that hurt, offend and upset those around us. The strange thing is, once we say we say we are sorry, there is often a remarkable transformation. We feel better and the person we have hurt also feels better. Apologising is a healing act, and it is as healing for us as it is for those to whom we apologise.

Saying we are sorry feels as if it will be an affront to our pride and as if it will make us less of a person, yet when we apologise, it opens the way for genuine feelings of self-worth to be restored. It may not happen at once, but it will come.

If we could think of being able to say we are sorry as the best way of living, perhaps we wouldn't resist it so much. When we refuse to apologise it is as if we are wrapping ourselves and the other person in heavy chains. Saying sorry breaks those chains and makes it possible for us to relate openly and freely again. Not apologising drains our energies and closes us down as people, as well as ruining relationships. It may be extremely difficult, but it is one of the most powerful things we can do to keep peace with ourselves, other people and God.

Another thing: when there has been a two-way offence, it is no good waiting for the other person to say sorry first. They may well be waiting for you to say sorry first, and then it becomes a pointless stalemate, with each of you continuing to nurse your offended feelings and living in that horrible fractured and damaged state. Be the one who initiates reconciliation and healing.

Saying we are sorry opens us up to being able to receive forgiveness from others and also allows us to forgive ourselves. Although we are assured that God has already forgiven us – that's part of what Jesus accomplished on the cross – it is still necessary to ask for forgiveness. Asking for forgiveness shows we recognise our need for it.

In common with being able to apologise, being able to forgive seems impossible at times. I don't believe it is necessary for us to be able to forgive all at once or even to know how to forgive, but what I think we have to do is to be *willing* to forgive, and then trust that God will show us how to do the rest when we are ready.

Letting Go

If Maundy Thursday is when we remember the watching and the praying, Jesus' dedication and commitment to do all that he knew he had come to do, then Good Friday is about both the final holding on, the sustained commitment, as well as about the final letting go. The faithfulness of Jesus on the cross, and his commending of himself into God's hands, shows us that we can also dare to place ourselves, our lives, our cares and concerns, into the waiting arms of a loving God.

There are times in life when we cannot hold on any longer. We've done our best and it's just too much. Letting go like this can be an act of faith, not a giving up. If we have placed ourselves into God's care, then we must wait for God to respond. Luke records the last words of Jesus on the cross as being 'Father, into your hands I commit my spirit' (Luke 23:46). If Jesus could trust God even as he died on the cross, then perhaps we can trust God with the concerns of our lives.

Moving On

We cannot possibly understand the totality of what happened on the cross, but we can believe that, as the late religious correspondent Gerald Priestland put it, whatever happened 'altered the moral chemistry of the universe.' Because of the cross, things are different, for us and for all of creation, for all time. Good Friday, and indeed all of Lent, is a good time for contemplating the ways in which the world was changed on the day Jesus died.

An aspect of what has changed is that we can live in a different kind of freedom, but it is a paradoxical freedom. When we embrace the freedom we have in Christ, our consciences become sensitised to an unimaginable degree and our hearts become attuned to the faintest, most feather-light caution of the Spirit. No chains or prison bars could ever hold a person in as effectively as the still small voice of the Spirit, when once a person becomes a disciple of Jesus Christ. We may not hear that voice every time it is spoken, but when we do, we know what we are called to do, down to the seemingly most insignificant detail of our lives.

We are indeed free – free from fear, free from bitterness and resentment, free to love, free to receive love – but friendship with the Holy Spirit demands an honesty and integrity and dedication that would be daunting were it not for the fact that the Spirit is the one who also makes it possible for us to hear and see and sense what we are being called to do and to be. As the prayer book collect puts it, 'without you we are not able to please you'.

By dying and rising again Jesus became the doorway to a new way of life for all people and all time. The unique and particular – a certain man at a certain time – transacted the universal means for the possibility of new life for all who can receive it. Pain and suffering are inescapable, and it is our attitude towards them that determines how we live our lives. The late John V. Taylor, former Bishop of Winchester once said that 'God is that deep-rooted pain within the universe from which love grows.' What a thought – love growing from pain, instead of love growing only from the sunny highlands of our lives.

Just as we trust that every year the flowers and buds and leaves and grain will grow again, so we can trust that whatever we do, whatever happens to us, God can renew our lives, revive our hopes, redeem our pasts. The way of Christ is through the cross, through death, but ultimately, the way of Christ is the way of Life.

FOR FURTHER THOUGHT
- What is most important to you about Jesus dying on the cross?
- Who do you most identify with in the story of the crucifixion?
- How would you choose to spend Good Friday? What can you do to make that happen?

FOR PRAYER
- Pray for people who endure constant pain and suffering.
- Pray for all those who are seeking truth.
- Pray to be shown anything for which you need to ask for forgiveness.

FOR FURTHER READING
- Matthew 27
- Mark 15
- Luke 23
- John 19
- Galatians 2:20–21
- Hebrews 12:1–2

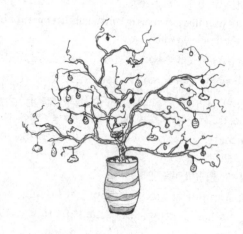

EASTER DAY

Jesus came and stood among them and said, 'Peace be with you'.

JOHN 20:19

The angel said to the women, 'Do not be afraid; for I know that you seek Jesus who was crucified. He is not here; for he has risen.'

MATTHEW 28:5–6

If you confess with your lips that Jesus is Lord and believe in your heart that God raised him from the dead, you will be saved.

ROMANS 10:9

If the Spirit of him who raised Jesus from the dead dwells in you, he who raised Christ Jesus from the dead will give life to your mortal bodies also through his Spirit which dwells in you.

ROMANS 8:11

The last enemy to be destroyed is death.

1 CORINTHIANS 15:26

For now is Christ risen.
He is risen! He is risen indeed! Alleluia!

Of all events in the life of Jesus, of all feasts and festivals in the Christian calendar, Easter is the greatest. Throughout the stretch of human history we have seen the repeated miracle of birth and we have witnessed the Spirit of God active in many circumstances and in many people's lives, but the events of the first Easter morning are unprecedented.

The resurrection is not about Jesus being resuscitated back into his old life. That would be a miracle in itself, but that's not what Easter is about. Easter is about God raising Jesus to a new kind of life, one in which we are invited to share by the power and presence of the Holy Spirit. Although we may not be able to do all the things that Jesus did after he had been resurrected, Jesus told us that we would be able to do even greater things once he had gone away and the Holy Spirit had been sent. He told his disciples that his leaving them would benefit them: 'Nevertheless, I tell you the truth: it is to your advantage that I go away, for if I do not go away the Spirit will not come to you; but if I go, I will send him to you' (John 16:7). Jesus promised that the Spirit would show the world what was right and what was wrong, and would lead them into all truth. They would not be left alone, desolate, without a guide.

The Holy Spirit was indeed sent, an event we celebrate on Pentecost Sunday, which comes fifty days after Easter. At Pentecost, Jesus' friends found themselves speaking in different languages and being able to heal people and perform other miracles. Perhaps most miraculously, Jesus' friends, who had been so demoralised and frightened after his death, became bold and fearless in their preaching, teaching and telling people about the wonderful news of God's love, given to everyone and shown in the life of the man whom they had known as a companion and friend.

Easter is the day for putting aside all the petty concerns and niggles of our lives and giving thanks for something we may believe to be wonderful, but we which we cannot begin to understand fully. The events of Easter are so amazing that we could spend our entire lives contemplating their significance. As far as possible, be at peace on this day above all days, and allow yourself to believe that the love and power of our good God is stronger than anything else in creation.

Suggestions for an Easter Feast

Make Easter a celebration from beginning to end. If it is appropriate, start with something special for breakfast, something you wouldn't ordinarily have, like Churchfield Eggs Benedict (p. 89), Keri's Old School Popovers (p. 92) or Kathy's splendid Galette (p. 93). Or if you wish to keep it simple, just have a soft-boiled egg or a dish of yogurt, nuts and honey.

My Easter menu usually consists of roast leg of lamb, roast white potatoes, sweet potatoes, parsnips, garlic and onions and we also have a few green vegetables, like broccoli, peas or specially cooked cabbage (see p. 138).

For pudding, I always make my grandmother's pascha (see p. 169).

Symbols of the Resurrection

Eggs are the oldest and most widespread symbol of the resurrection. They speak of new life and of transformation. The hard enclosed shell reveals a living, breathing fluffy chick. Something which is entirely closed and complete is broken and enables a new life to begin. In Orthodox Churches Easter eggs are dyed red, to symbolise the blood Jesus shed on the cross. The shell of the egg is seen as the sealed tomb, which is then cracked – a sign of the resurrection.

The peacock is a symbol of the resurrection in China and elsewhere. Every year the male peacock loses all two hundred of his splendid eye feathers, and every year new ones grow. This dramatic display of growth, loss and re-growth is also a sign of immortality. The feathers always re-grow, just as life always wins over death.

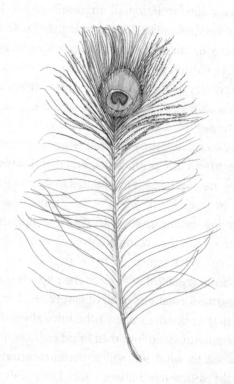

The butterfly is a particularly fitting symbol for Easter. It represents new life, transformation, or an imminent breakthrough. Though we see butterflies as fragile and their lives as fleeting, they symbolise the ability to undergo significant change and to adapt to a new form of life. Although small and delicate, butterflies are actually amazingly resilient and strong: some species migrate thousands of miles each year.

The butterfly goes through four distinct stages of growth: the egg, larva, pupa and finally, the exquisite winged creature. In the larval stage, the butterfly is essentially a caterpillar. It eats a lot and sheds its skin a number of times. It has to shed its skin to make room for its increase in size. Then, when it is a pupa, the butterfly undergoes a stunning metamorphosis. During this stage the cells are actually disassembled and then completely reassembled, in readiness for the final stage. What emerges from the cocoon bears no resemblance to the caterpillar that entered the pupa. It is one of the most spectacular transformations in all of nature.

Could it be that in the life cycle of the butterfly we can see a parable about the potentiality of our own lives? Is life here on planet earth, as compared to what we will experience after death, as improbable as the difference between the larva and the adult butterfly? There are certainly things about our own existence that we simply cannot fathom, not because we are not extraordinarily intelligent and perceptive creatures, but because there are things that are simply outside our present ability to conceive.

Astrophysicists can explain with a high degree of certainty things that are happening in the far-flung reaches of space, things that cannot be studied through a telescope. At times they have to use a deductive process: in order for such and such to make sense, such and such needs to be happening. If the universe behaves the way it does, then certain things need to be taking place.

If some people were to come upon a butterfly, having never seen or heard about the process of the butterfly's development, even with careful observation they would never arrive at the correct understanding of how it grows.

The frustrating fact is that we can't know what we don't know. We cannot step outside our own boundaries of perception, however large they may be, and imagine something entirely incomprehensible to our understanding.

This is why I think atheists are skating on thin ice. To state categorically that there is no God is a rather presumptuous claim. We know an awful lot about our universe, and we are discovering more all the time, but we are no closer to knowing the *why*: *why* did the Big Bang happen? How did whatever it was that existed before any matter existed come to have the potential to create this universe? How do we know that this universe could not have been created by an eternal Being who has always been and will always be, and whose primary mode of existence is in a different dimension to the one we happen to find ourselves mostly living in at the moment? We certainly know enough to know there is much we do not know.

I can well understand why some people are agnostic. I think it is entirely reasonable to wonder, to question and to doubt. I get a bit worried by people of faith who never allow for the possibility that they could just be very wrong about some things. Just as there is an intellectual arrogance and assumption on the part of atheists, there is also a type of spiritual arrogance that sits uncomfortably in the life of a true believer. Faith does not require absolute proof of the veracity of one's beliefs. Faith strives for wisdom, clarity, understanding and truth, but it does not demand proof of the divine and the dimensions of the spirit in terms that, inevitably, are bound to be convincing to human perception.

I would hate to have to take on Richard Dawkins, because I expect he could run rings around me with his breadth of knowledge about our universe, but, for all that he knows, Richard Dawkins can never know what I know. He does not understand what I have seen and felt and experienced – and he cannot fully know what I believe. All his dogmatic unbelief can never take away my faith and my perception of life and the universe.

I am sure that I could learn a great deal from Dawkins about this marvellous universe, but I cannot learn from him about the things of the spirit, because he does not accept that there is a spiritual dimension to our beings and he has no interest in pursuing the possibility that there is more to life that what can ultimately be measured, observed and understood in rational and scientific terms.

In a sense, it is as if the Dawkins of this world are insisting that only a certain type of bridge (rational, scientific knowledge) is valid for trying to span a certain type of chasm (all the facts about the universe that we still don't know). Even more than that, it is as if the atheistic rationalists are stating that they already know certain things about what will and will not be discovered on the far side of the chasm. This is a strange attitude for a scientist, because certainly one of the most striking things that scientists and theologians have in common is a desire to discover the truth. That desire, and the awareness of the incompleteness of our present knowledge, should keep us open, inquisitive – and humble.

Blaise Pascal, the great French polymath of the seventeenth century, wrote a famous defence for belief in God in spite of the impossibility of proving the existence of God. His rationale has become known as Pascal's wager. Pascal acknowledges that whether or not God exists is something that cannot be proved by reason. He then weighs the relative gains and losses of betting on God's existence.

As he puts it, if you live and behave as if God exists, and it turns out that God does exist, then 'you win everything; if you lose, you lose nothing'. In other words, a life lived according to Christian principles and the decision to believe in a loving God results in a virtuous and rewarding life in and of itself.

In his letter to the Christians at Corinth, Paul acknowledges the limits of knowledge – even the special knowledge that comes as a gift from God – and contrasts this with the superior virtues of faith, hope and love. The Amplified Version of the Bible expresses it in this way:

Love never fails – never fades out or becomes obsolete or comes to an end. As for prophecy (that is, the gift of interpreting the divine will and purpose), it will be fulfilled and pass away (that is, it will lose its value and be superseded by truth).

For our knowledge is fragmentary (incomplete and imperfect), and our prophecy (our teaching) is fragmentary (incomplete and imperfect). But when the complete and perfect (total) comes, the incomplete and imperfect will vanish away – become antiquated, void and superseded.

When I was a child, I talked like a child, I thought like a child, I reasoned like a child; now that I have become a man, I am done with childish ways and have put them aside.

For now we are looking in a mirror that gives only a dim (blurred) reflection (of reality as in a riddle or enigma), but then (when perfection comes) we shall see in reality and face to face! Now I know in part (imperfectly); and then I shall know and understand fully and clearly, even in the same manner as I have been fully and clearly known and understood (by God).

And so faith, hope and love abide; (faith, conviction and belief respecting people's relation to God and divine things; hope, joyful and confident expectation of eternal salvation; love, true affection for God and humanity, growing out of God's love for and in us), these three, but the greatest of these is love.

1 CORINTHIANS 13:8–13

Paul's awareness of the limitations of our knowledge made no difference to what he believed, but the two great events of Jesus' life and of Lent – the crucifixion and the resurrection – were essential to Paul in order to make sense of his faith.

Paul, who never knew Jesus when Jesus was alive on earth, initially became obsessed with stamping out the beliefs in Jesus that sprang up around him. Then he was blinded by Christ as he hurried to Damascus, hoping to discover and arrest more of the followers of the man who had claimed to be the son of God. As a result of that encounter Paul became one of the most fearless followers of Jesus Christ. Paul would eventually go to his death rather than deny the one who had revealed himself as the risen Christ.

The events surrounding the resurrection were of crucial importance to Paul. Paul's absolute assurance in the forgiveness of sins and the possibility of eternal life hung on the reality of the resurrection. In fact, Paul reasoned, if there is no resurrection and being a Christian is of value only in this life, then, as he put it, 'we are of all people most miserable and to be pitied' (1 Corinthians 15:19, Amplified Version).

I do not think he could have gone along with the cool logic of Pascal and his wager. For Paul, his faith stood or fell on the reality of the resurrection of Jesus Christ. After the encounter with Christ on the road to Damascus, Paul never doubted. He had been met and blinded by the living Christ, whose followers he was busy rounding up and having put to death.

My own faith is not based on such a dramatic conversion. I was raised by a mother and father who already believed, but at some point I had to carry on believing for myself. I expect that most people who take a step of faith do so for many and various reasons, and such a step is rarely based on knowledge or facts alone. Both the logic of Pascal's wager and the didactic certainty of Dawkins' atheism fade into a mist when faced with an experience of the living Christ.

The bottom line is that God knows and we don't. What is important is to be aware of things about yourself and your life, about other people, living and dead, that bring you to a point of realising there is *more*. There is more to life than we can see and touch and smell and taste and hear, however good all those things may be. There is more than what we can observe and measure. It is like the astrophysicists, deciding what has to be happening in space because of what is else is also happening in space. It is like the little poem by Christina Rossetti we learned as children:

> Who has seen the wind?
> Neither I nor you.
> But when the leaves hang trembling,
> the wind is passing through.
> Who has seen the wind?
> Neither you nor I.
> But when the trees bow down their heads,
> the wind is passing by.

Some people live lives that clearly resemble trees that have been shaped by the wind. And when hundreds of millions of people over two thousand years all seem to have a certain similarity of shape, blown in a way that has become strangely familiar, then perhaps it is a wise and safe choice to walk with these people, facing in the same direction – and wait for the wind to blow.

FOR FURTHER THOUGHT
- What does the resurrection of Jesus Christ mean to me?
- What in my life needs to be transformed?
- In what way do I understand myself to be part of a new creation?

FOR PRAYER

- Pray that you might know the joy of the resurrection in your own life.
- Pray the same prayer for other people.
- Pray for all people who need the restoring power of hope in their lives.

FOR FURTHER READING

The stories of the resurrection in the Gospels:

- John 20:1ff
- Luke 24:1ff
- Mark 16:1ff
- Matthew 28:1ff

THREE BLESSINGS

May the roots of faith grow strong within you.
May your vision of peace be like a clear sky.
May you be touched by the lightning flash of bright hope.
May you drink deeply at the well of joy.
May the love of God
be your blanket and your pillow,
your bed and your room,
and may God's arms surround you
now and for ever more.
Amen.

Love is divine power.
Divine power is love.

May the power of divine love
fill you, protect you and give you peace,
now and always.
Amen.

The LORD bless you and keep you:
the LORD make his face to shine upon you and be gracious to you:
the LORD turn his face towards you, and give you peace.

NUMBERS 6:24–26

And the peace of God, which surpasses all understanding, will guard
your hearts and your minds in Christ Jesus.

PHILIPPIANS 4:7

INDEX OF RECIPES